THE MODEST AUDACITY BLESSING OF LOVE

or

THE Oy VEY GEVALT CHUTZPAH BURDEN OF LUST!

NORAH G. WILSON

Copyright © 2021 by Norah G. Wilson

Paperback: 978-1-63767-382-9
eBook: 978-1-63767-383-6

All rights reserved. No part of this publication may be reproduced, distributed, or transmitted in any form or by any electronic or mechanical means, without the prior written permission of the publisher, except in the case of brief quotations embodied in critical reviews and certain other noncommercial uses permitted by copyright law.

This is a work of nonfiction.

Ordering Information:

BookTrail Agency
8838 Sleepy Hollow Rd.
Kansas City, MO 64114

Printed in the United States of America

TABLE OF CONTENTS

Prologue v

Chapter 1   If it's "THE WILL OF THE SPIRIT"
            we will do this or that! 1
Chapter 2   Brother & Sister's Chutzpah! 6
Chapter 3   The House Built On Oy Vey Lust! 10
Chapter 4   The Audacity of Divinity! 14
Chapter 5   There is a Time For Love! 17
Chapter 6   Chains that Bind With Lust of Hate! 21
Chapter 7   Oy Vey Gevalt Chutzpah! 24
Chapter 8   The Sister Pushed Aside! 29
Chapter 9   A House Divided Cannot Tolerate Peace 33
Chapter 10 Inlove With My Dreaman! 39
Chapter 11 Within My Soul I Knew You! 46
Chapter 12 A Dreaman WOKE Me Up 50

Epilogue 55
Word Definition 59
Summary 71
Authors Notes 75
About The Author 77
Special Spiritual Thanks 79

PROLOGUE

There is a chilling boldness of impudence, disrespecting the 18 senses of the very proud and self-willed; an audacity that overcomes the mind ruling the sensors subjected to time, chance and change.

This audacity is "divinity!" What is Divinity? Divinity is the attribute of being "Divine;" Divine is the unbridled involuntary will that controls the destination of time and changes in life and death. This is why we are never to promise or swear; we cannot control time neither change what is or will not happen or change what Divinity chooses what, where to who it will; when it will, at will! "Divinity" is the "Will" that changes and makes up *your mind*!

"Divinity" has no mind to change, it is "Will" "Divinity" never thinks, it knows; this "Divine Will" is permanent and unchangeable! This divine will never hesitates or stumbles or makes mistakes to change its will; the mind thinks because it doesn't know what the divine will do in time to change the chances of the future!

"Divinity" is the surreal and mind-blowing audacious will! "This Divine Will" roots out, plucks up and plants a foundation for those that are "predestined and spiritually conceived *"inlove"* An unmindful, unretentive, unmerciful will of correction, goes unchangeable as time obeys *"THE MODEST BLESSING OF THE AUDACITY OF LOVE!"*

There are "2 spiritual Wills;" *"DIVINE AND PERMISSIVE"* Permit means to allow; but this permissiveness is only chronological, "ENABLINGING OR ALLOWING YOU TO DO WHAT YOU WANT OR SEE FIT ON YOUR OWN CHOOSING OR VOLUNTARY ACTION."

Permissiveness is, but for a season; allowing a change for the better or worse which is another way to look at it being a "Permissive ill!"

This "Permissive ill" works basically along with the law of convenience! During emergencies and grief and sudden calamities, relief from these things that would cause undue stress and burdens of hardships is given just for a set time, or until "The fullness of time!" The perfect scripture in the King James version is *"It rains on the just as well as the unjust, but he gives me shelter in the time of storm." The divine will not stop the storm and will not stop the rain, but you are permitted an umbrella to walk to shelter. Let's trust you remembered to bring the umbrella, or did you think it wasn't going to rain even when you saw the dark clouds? Remember procrastination is a sin!*

This may or may not be what would be a comfortable thing for you, but this "permissive ill" is going to make or break you! It is a good thing to love and honor your parents that begat you; this the first promise made to a child for a very foundation of life, but this is the stumbling block most people become failures in life as disobedient children.

Of course *life* is a *lesson*; but the rules began with the hand that provided for us, and the devotion to give back and not bite the hand that fed us. There is a reward for the child that obeys it's *parents* and a punishment for the disobedient as well. A young prince is guarded and obeys his father and mother, but a heathen runs free and knows no correction, neither will he regard correction and soon runs into mischief. There is a "Will" that seeks TO KEEP SAFE its own, and an "ill" that seeks to REJECT AND destroy; the circuit of the order of the day is "THE MODEST BLESSING OF THE AUDACITY OF LOVE OR THE OY VEY GEVALT CHUTZPAH OF LUST!"

WE ARE ALL COUNTED AS SHEEP FOR THE SLAUGHTER; KILLED ALL DAY LONG, BUT ONE SHALL BE TWO AND THEY SHALL BE JOINED INLOVE; NOTHING SHALL BY ANY MEANS HURT THEM. Touch not my anointed and do my prophets no harm; *those joined in a conception of "inlove" are the "anointed" of the spirit! Truly the man that is given his spiritual wife is blessed and highly favored, dwelling in a secret place of the most high. A long life will be given them, showing them the mighty divine will of the spirit.*

CHAPTER ONE

If it's
"THE WILL OF THE SPIRIT"
we will do this or that!

Isn't it peculiar how we can be so determined in attempting what we want, without thinking about the temptations involved?

I must say from the experience of my own motherhood, infants don't think; all were conceived in a demand to order style.

The sperm has a driving will, and the egg has patience to wait, resulting in the beginning of each conception joining in the chance of time.

I sit looking out my window listening to baby birds chirping in nests, blending with the singing of the adult birds. I think some of the things I know have finished its course in love and lust; some things I will not mention. *Why do you need to know? You knowing about it would not have changed or stopped the divine will of the spirit!*

The divine will does not repent or make errors; the divine will is not persuaded or charmed or to be pleaded with! There is only one will of the divine; the faith of the chosen shall live by the divine will and walk not by sight but by the light of truth which shines upon the pathway in the divine will! Few shall find this path; it's not paved in stone, or lined with gold, but is in the soul of those that are joined inlove!

I shake my head over the many directions that led down the wrong paths. Love is never lust and lust is never love; love does not love lust, but lust lusts after love, both working from the hypothalamus gland, but the divine will controls the hypothalamus gland! Lust gives out over time, but love works as long as the heart beats!

Years ago before I was born, there was a woman who met and married a soldier; never had children, yet they lived happily married until death separated them.

This couple was married years by the time I met them growing up; they both would inspire me even though my many marriages had repeatedly failed over and over again. She told me once how "Bucky" was so good to her; that was her nickname for her husband of over 40 years, being so kind and understanding.

I visited their home; such a sweet peace welcomed me there. Bucky would smile lovingly at his wife; she would pass certain glances back and forth to him; I as a young teenager not realizing the memory would never be forgotten.

This couple reached old age together; both developed diabetes but cared for one another. The wife woke up early one morning to find Bucky slumped over in his favorite chair.

At first glance, Bucky appeared to be sleeping; "good morning dear" she greeted him thinking he would open his eyes from sleep as she rushed up to kiss him on his forehead. It seemed odd to her that he didn't respond. Yet upon a closer look, the wife noticed Bucky's dentures had fallen into his lap; then with a sudden ache within her chest, she knew something was so very wrong.

The woman touched her husband's side as they both appeared to be slumped over with both of their heads together; Bucky was not breathing! Her heart gripped her from deep inside; a force with an emptiness that she had never known before now, she was *alone* in a dark place. *The joint conception between them had been broken, her Bucky was dead!*

The dear woman told me this sad story as she went on with her life, alone. She moved in with her sister who was younger than her, yet she too had diabetes; these two sisters were the oldest of 3, their youngest sister lived out of the city in another state.

The years seemed to pass with a darkness within and without; the old woman of 80 plus years became imprisoned to her handicap body. Sorrows, pains, griefs, blindness, bound her to a wheelchair with one amputated leg; she was a burden preying on the mercy of her sister.

The 2 sisters converted the home into a convalescent home where they continued the rest of their lives together.

The older sister became a burden to her sister; overhearing her sister make the remark, "when her husband died, she was going to travel and enjoy her life."

The older sister never asked to come live with her sister; her sister asked her to live in her home after making her oldest sister power of attorney over all her money Bucky had labored and willed her.

The middle sister reconstructed the home, making an investment without a day nurse or any outside professional help in the comfort of the convalescence of her oldest sister.

Not all the money went into this house, her sister had other plans! Time became a burden to the older sister who only went out of the house on Sundays attending church where she gave tithes and offerings. The Pastor never paid home visits but sent the Church bus every service to pick her up. No one knew how the grieved woman desired to just "*go home* with Bucky!"

Her sister planned on going to Las Vegas after putting her away in a nursing home to enjoy life. The years took its toll on both sisters, at times neither thought they would make it through the night with threatening high glucose and blood pressure readings.

Suddenly one day there came a long distance call alerting the middle sister that her grandson was rushed to the hospital due to a fall in his blood sugar owing to his diabetes...

The middle sister hurried into town checking her oldest sister into a nearby nursing home, then went to the airport claiming her seat on the *red eye* to Las Vegas.

This was not what she had planned; but then never mind trying to fool the tricks of time or the "Divine Will!" Nothing was going to prepare her for the "Divine Will" that has no mind to change or even a shadow of turning back the hands of time!

Time was ticking as she rushed out of the airport in the state where she called the cab to take her to the hospital just as her daughter called with the news of her grandson's passing. *The divine will showed no mercy*; there was no grace or margin for a plea bargain on her grandson's life by the Pastor, the divine will had been done!

Shock flowed through the sister's body as she entered the doors of the family room where her daughter swept her into her arms with violent sobs.

The daughter later drove her mother to her house when a call came from another state as soon as they entered the house. Her mother's younger sister's daughter was on the phone, it was strange that this niece would be calling this late!

The grieving grandmother was having trouble hearing what her niece was saying as silently her blood pressure rose within her veins. She listened to her niece "I'm sorry Auntie, but mama just died!" "Oy Vey!" This sister lived in Indiana, the youngest of the three sisters!

She nearly dropped the phone trying to hold onto her own daughter for support standing next to her who looked grief stricken with the loss of her only son just hours before.

There was no comfort in the voice that came over the phone; the niece repeated the same words, they meant the same things "Auntie, my mama; your baby sister just died! She heard her Niece the first time, yet the second time only made the pain worse!

She thought to herself as she felt her blood pressure begin to drain every ounce of energy from her body; stress dropped her sugar in her veins, suddenly she could not take all this stress!

Nevertheless, over the course of the next 12 days both funeral arrangements were made; however, she made it to her grandson's funeral in Las Vegas, but missed her own sister's funeral in Indiana! The middle sister was drained by the weekend; she took a flight back to the home where she opened the door to an empty house; suddenly the room went black. A neighbor saw the open door with the middle sister laying on the floor!

The middle sister was admitted to the nearby nursing home; a room, an empty bed, was assigned waiting for her. *The "Divine Will"* preserved the strength of the oldest sister who, laying in the darkness, heard her middle sister's name mentioned from the nurse who checked on both sisters sharing the same hospice care!

5 months later, the middle sister took a grave turn for the worse; died in her sleep as the blind amputated older sister held on to the ebbs of life while seeing the light at the end of the tunnel getting closer to her being beamed up, but by the *"permissive will _____ "* she waited!

The funeral services were nearly over; the family lingering at the graveyard when the deceased sister's daughter again received a call from the nursing home; the oldest sister just died as the casket of her 2nd sister was being lowered into her grave, all 3 sisters died within 6 months of one another! Oy Vey gevalt chutzpah!

The niece remembered the words her auntie spoke to her not even a year ago; she was going to travel when her husband died and put her sister in a nursing home, now she is dead, my aunt had a burden of lust!

I remember a lot of things about those 3 sisters; the oldest 2 were my Aunties, the youngest of the 3 sisters was my mama!

The one thing that stood out about the oldest sister was this; she always spoke of the love between her and Bucky.

Bucky had been dead for over 20 years at this time of sharing, but my Auntie blind and helpless, shared these memories; happy treasured moments talking to me about her and Bucky being inlove.

My aunt and uncle Bucky had a blessing of love! *The audacity of faith* that had her outlive her sisters who never had the conception of being joined inlove with one man! She never had children with Bucky, but they had the *fountain of youth together*!

That was her favorite subject and the only thing that seemed to keep her alive was the love that she had even after death took the body away from her husband; they still were joined by their spirits that cannot die!

I grew up realizing this couple touched my life; somehow meant to prove to me that very few people together were "inlove!"

CHAPTER TWO

Brother & Sister's Chutzpah!

I watched everyone around me, beginning within my mama's house; there was no love to be found, only charred bits and pieces of lust that marked its victims for life!

There was lies being lived between them; every family member was living a lie of some sort beginning with who they say they loved, but there is a difference between lust, and being "inlove!"

This was what I saw; I began to accept what I thought was love for myself as well. Love despised me I thought; what I thought I knew about this kind of love could not be trusted, it never lasted or so I thought!

I was wrong, all wrong; and so were everyone else that believed that love "hurts!" It was lust all along that not only hurts but leaves us deceived and scarred; the consequences for being led by our own personal sensors that blink in and out of darkness.

I closed my eyes to everyone around me in their miseries; I had my own disasters stumbling in the directions where my 18 senses led me, and *"the permissive will"* allowed me to make what I thought were good choices in my life! Little did I understand the divine will does not "mind" the lust that the world is founded upon. The divine will is not persuaded or charmed by wants and sacrifices; I didn't understand why I was born and why my real father didn't love me and the list only enlarged from there! I felt humbled; that was not a good feeling. The spirit gives grace to the humble and abase the proud.

I had so much to learn from other people's misfortunes, yet it never helped me in the mistakes I fell prey to. I knew better than to sleep around with the boys in my neighborhood that seemed to follow any females like bees buzzing around flowers. They all wanted a sample of the nectar that seemed to give off a sensor to detect where the honey was!

I truly believed in marriage; holding on to my virginity until my wedding night was something I would do. I watched this one family; the 2 oldest girls were very pretty, and all the boys pursued them.

Somehow, I didn't understand why they would be so sneaky behind their parents' backs. I later learned each of the oldest sisters were being molested by their stepfather and what an awful story this turned out to be.

How could their mother not see what was going on right under her nose with her own husband and her children? She was blinded; what blinded the mother? Lust!

Needless to say, the permissive will allow everyone their choice; they chose to close their eyes to the matter and go along with the evils that lurked inside the lust that held them captive to one another's unseen evils! There are signs that read "travel at your own risk," but there are risks when one uses their 18 senses which are undiscerning spiritual things like love without being given the gift of "faith!"

The mother mistook kindness for pretense; kindness distracted and covered weakness in a man that had no strength for empathy.

People led by lust learn how to put on a happy face and say the right words only for a while; when lust removes its cover to expose the dark evilness of contempt, the face is distorted into a mask of rage.

Babies natural involuntary actions is life sustaining but learning to use their brains with their 18 senses is a manipulate skill developing into manipulating first the mother then the rest of the family, but a father can put a stop to this behavior before the child learns to use his skills of his 18 senses to manipulate the rest of the world around him.

The sisters got off to a bad start in life as the leader of a mother that also had a bad start in her young life as well. Molestation: is it the act of pestering or harassing a young age child sexually out of curiosity or because one or both persons were immature, or an older senseless lawless person was trusted around a child that should not have been?

I know the first thing that came to your mind was "sexual" misconduct with a minor is always done by a person that wants to be devivent; this may very well end up being the case with a minor.

Children learn by curiosity, this begins with themselves, then they are curious with everyone else; but this is why mothers need to be with their child to see them. You can't watch a child if you don't see them! Where are the "mamas" when their child is molested?" Were they in the wrong place, or watching the wrong thing?

Long before any act is committed; the thought begins within the heart that is led by as far as the eyes can see and what is within their reach at the moment.

Just like babies, what they see, they want to reach out to touch; but just to touch is not good enough, it must be grasped with the fingers and then everything touched aims to the mouth; but everything we put in our mouth is not good to eat.

Again, everything we see is not to be reached for, touched or to be had; some children get older, but they never seem to learn the rule at the museum when in kindergarten. Look, but don't touch; they never learned to restrain themselves to not reach out and touch a person without permission! A child is taught at home, by their parents the basic things; their bodies are private, not public!

I have begun to tell you about a family but let me tell you about the man that molested his stepchildren, both 2 little 8- and 9-year-old sisters and their little brother of 7!

This was the unthinkable thing, but this man did what he did because he lusted after a deep-seated desire that longed to be satisfied then it turned to resentment then to a deep-seated anger!

This desire was always making itself known to not just this one man in particular, but to me as well as you!

This desire is to be loved! You want to be loved; I desire to be loved. This man was not wrong to desire affection, but what he did to get affection was wrong!

The world is full of this desire, full of unfulfilled by the wrong people, places and things! What do you do to satisfy that longing that is not fulfilled by being inlove? I'm not talking about what you let people know about, it's what you do when you're hurt inside and you can't face the world? Do you drink, fight, become a workaholic, or do you have a secret lust?

Do you just fill your life with the woes of others till you can't find the time to even care about being all alone in this world without being inlove?

Let's just follow the lives of this man and this woman and the family that only wanted to love and be loved in return, but lust ruined the lives of all that followed after their 18 senses!

CHAPTER THREE

The House Built On Oy Vey Lust!

The mother of the 2 girls was not always a mother; she once was a small child, once preyed upon by her stepfather.

She kept this secret to herself and took it all in stride as she did with her 2nd husband; she didn't have trust with her 1st husband, yet in lust, there is never any trust intended; lust is free to give to anyone you care to give it to!

Lust everyone; but being inlove is not a party, it's just for those that are spiritually joined. Lust is a hot desire that is never satisfied; it's like a virus that spreads from person to person and even groups of places ____ a wildfire that is burning out of control.

Just for fun or just because you were drunk, or angry or for whatever comes to mind that your senses suddenly wanders from place to place. Beauty is only skin deep; lust gets under the skin like a poison ivy rubbing you the wrong way; your hypothalamus sends out an *"itch sense"* alert to your immune system to get rid of that strange thing that is not a part of your body! Lust can make you sick, tired and even kill you; but before it consumes you, it works on your 18 senses!

The mother wanted to just be held; this lust seduced her into the dark web that weaved her 3 children into being molested like her, captive in their own minds from guilt and shame for the rest of their lives.

I only wish this were the only horror of lust, it is not; what one sees is not all there is to be seen, lust is a spirit that only pretends to be what it cannot be. Lust wants to be love; but love won't allow it to be soul!

I believe it is proper to explain to you as my reader this one truth; there is more than what appears to the eyes. There is something that each and every one of us, you and I have; we have our essence that projects a barrier of who we are.

We cannot alter who we really are inside our bodies. We are all true to ourselves, yet that does not mean that we will ever let anyone know the true person we are except to the one that is joined in the spirit of oneness of ourselves.

Everyone does not have and will not be given this gift! To be *awakened* to being *"inlove"* is one of the most thrill I ever known! *To know that we both know it happened is beyond words,* just a joy unspeakable and full of glory and beyond anything either could ask or think! We know that we are inlove and this love is a gift we treasure together every day for the rest of our lives together!

Only being inlove is the reflection of oneself's desires. We live in a world where everything is only in a form that appears to be something that is misleading, deceptive…

We see something that appeals to our curiosity and when we touch it, we only are drawn to taste and just one more sensory thing and we may find ourselves in a situation that is far from happiness and nothing to do with love and truthfulness.

Who is this child molester? He himself molested even when he was a child. The vicious cycle repeats itself in a circuit of unrepented, unforgivable seeds planted in children; tender plants that became rooted in the stony dregs of fear, doubt and unbelief of lust.

I won't give this man a name, lust has many given names or titles of its own; I will just let you know him by his character of lust.

Lust's character is flawed; it has a vain self-esteem, the desire to be appreciated and admired by others while boosting the ego and pride of themselves. This really is something that all men have, they all are born with the trait to be dominant. Don't get me wrong, there's nothing wrong with every male being dominant, but he can only dominate what is his to have!

Testosterone is the driving force within the shell of the body of a man; it is the drive of the male and the force of his body to dominate, but only one female will summit one man's dominance for life!

This man is comparable to any other man looking for a place in this world to call his own while guarding his possessions with a gun; if he felt necessary, he'd kill to keep others away. It's only the lust of the eyes, flesh and pride of life that bare ills common to all of us giving nothing of satisfaction without the downside!!

Every little boy needs a balance in his life that is only shared between his parents and him; this balance is the deoxyribonucleic acid between the 3 of them in this world.

The matter is, this boy has both his parents ``deoxyribonucleic acid," but the parents never share their deoxyribonucleic together except through their child in a chemical conception which will not make any man or woman be joined "inlove" with one another!

The electrical circuit of joining inlove did not exist between his father and his mother; being the real *conception* that *joins* a man and a woman to be *inlove* for life before they join their bodies in intercourse and before the conception of their deoxyribonucleic acid that made them parents of a child...

His parents were just *inlust* together for a short time; but there was an evil that haunted them in the phantom of lust for a lifetime!

Not just any man or woman can be inlove; even having sex and making deoxyribonucleic acid blend together between the nucleus of the sperm and the egg is not permitted to join the parents to be "inlove" or even to make "love!"

Love is not made by two people; love is given to both as a gift! Love is spiritually divinely, given to two people and they exquisitely, delightfully and beautifully physically share it together for their remaining lifetime!

Love is given to a man and a woman and both know who they are and are aware of the joy between them without telling the other! Lust just happens everywhere; lurking around where the divine will will not be. *Love is a conception of the spirit guiding two people together permanently. Lust is a contraption of the physical opposites deceiving with their forms for earthly gain.*

We all have just one pair of maternal and paternal parents; no one can have more than 2 mothers or fathers. Another truth whether we believe or not; out of over 960 million people in the world, there is only one person in this number that you can ever be joined-spiritually inlove with for life! You cannot choose your conception of love any more than you could have the choice of who your parents would be in your own body's conception in your mother's womb, or the deoxyribonucleic acid of your blood-type or the timing of your puberty!

There is a time for everything; to be born there is a set time, to love there is a time for love; but it's not your making it happen!

The majority of all maternal and paternal parents were not meant to be parents together because they never experienced the result of a "spiritual conception" that is also electrical through a circuit beyond our control called "inlove!"

Will you be able to understand how life without the male and female uniting together as one conception inlove is nothing more than lust; in time they will erode becoming just a sad story?

You think that once you see something you want, you can have it; but you are in for a big surprise! What you see is not what you get!

We are made to look alike somewhat, but we are not alike. From this unique oneness, the same uniqueness of a joining comes into action when you are joined; "inlove!"

CHAPTER FOUR

The Audacity of Divinity!

Let me go on telling you the story of this misfortunate, pathetic boy that grew up to be a wicked, unagi stepfather; only searching for something he would never find because it was never lost!

You just may wrestle and grapple with memories of dried skeletons hidden in closets of your family as well, while denying the light of day behind your shaded glasses!

He was warped in his tender years; there are things children should never see, never hear, and never feel, or smell or taste.

Our 18 senses are not to pick out our life partners, but to warn us somewhat of the dangers lurking around us and stay balanced and walk in a straight path, taste the difference between salty, bitter, sweet or yuck!

Eyes get dim and even get dust in them and even go blind where we can't see whether it's dark or light; our hearing may go bad as well so as we can't hear sound vibrations in water or the air. As with any of our 18 senses leaving us mentally senile and unsane without them. You do know that it's our 18 senses that qualify us to be sane? Yes I did mean 18 and not 5 or 6! Of course you may not be dealing with a full sense about you, but with whatever amount of senses you use, what can you do without them? What would you do if you were born without your 18 senses? You would not be able to relate to anything; the world only is here as you can sense it! No sense, no world! Still following the early life of this young boy; it was a Sunday summer day as he rode beside his paternal and maternal parents on their way to the neighborhood church.

Even though his father and mother were lawfully permitted to live together and have children, even as a child, he understood there was a strange distant feeling cooling between them. Lust is never the same and never means to stay, but it comes around and stirs up jealousy. Lust is the imitation of love!

The young boy lived with this sense of tension all of his childhood; his muscles tensed and he could feel the nociception censoring in his bones something was never just right between them two, but this was not the straw that broke the camel's back.

Every Sunday his dad would drop him and his mother off at church; then leave only to return to pick us up after services.

He saw what his dad never saw; oh he didn't see much, it was what he didn't see that made him angry and confused, for the remainder of his life; little did he understand how his sense of discernment was working, but this was a spiritual sense common to blood type O people!

What was it that the young boy became confused over? It was something that planted a seed; the power of suggestion of doubt when his mother disappeared once inside the empty church.

There was always the door that closed behind her and the pastor giving him the element of surprise that there was a service going on in the back of the Church behind closed doors.

The boy never saw anything to come to a conclusion; but when his mother did finally join the congregation, her smile was something that I noticed. It was not so much of what was seen, but more of what he could not see that made his discernment sensor work over time!

Mama looked happy; she would give off this radiance that even a blind man could see, she tried to not look at the pastor's wife when she came in and took the front seat.

The pastor's wife was all dolled up in her vanities; that high feathered hat and fancy clothes, but she lacked the sparkle mama and that Pastor always had in their eyes. The kind of smile that neither knew was on their faces when they thought no one was watching, but was there plain as day!

Mama somehow tried to hide her smile when dad came to pick us up; if I looked close into her eyes, I would see the glow of love.

Her eyes smiled, but she simply seemed to close up like a flower when the sun went down, only to open when it rose up the next day under the warmth of the sun.

The Pastor seemed to be mama's sunshine lighting up her eyes! She just couldn't help it; she was inlove, following her heart and the hell with what people would think!

The little boy was not stupid, but dumb. Stupid to think that his mama and dad being married by law made a big difference in making the two of them special. This was not going unnoticed even to a child that kept silent.

Love is not lust and neither is lust love. The "Divine Will" connects, joins; the beginning of the circuits flowing between just one blood type"O" man and one blood type "O" woman!

This is the true union of being one together; Without the "Divine Will" being "inlove is impossible! Only through the "Devine Willing "Spiritual Inlove Conception will one man be one circuit with one woman! Being " joined" is simply connecting the electrical circuit in the blood type "O" man and one blood type "O" woman creating a berserk connection between them; they now are conceived in a love conception as a new creation!

Unbelievable until this "Spiritual Conception" transpires you! Love is love and lust is lust; there is no halfway ground in-between, either you're inlove or you're not! Love has no mutations! The blood type O has no mutations! Being "inlove" is based upon a blood-type, but it's more than being the same blood type O; it's being conceived to be together in a certain time of life by a power of the divine will to remain "inlove for the remainder of both lives!

Either 2 are joined inlove or they are just physically lusting and wanting something more than they are permitted to ever have together. Being inlove is spiritually divinely given involuntarily resisting time chance or change for the better and good for the remainder of both lives.

Lust is something you physically or lawfully consciously voluntarily take temporarily at your own risk of time chance and changes falling prey to the chutzpah in life!

CHAPTER FIVE

There is a Time For Love!

Dumb to the fact there was something his mama and the pastor had; he would never be gifted with a woman. Things seemed all very wrong to him; understanding through a few of his 18 senses bewitching him of a narrow minded view of his mama.

The little boy watched his mother until one day time changed things forever. It was one Sunday as it appeared to be like any other Sunday in the past, but this Sunday time made a change that made life different.

His dad never lived to come back to pick his mama and him up again. There was a fatal accident that claimed the life of his father; the husband of lust and law-marriage with his mother was killed!

The little boy was only 8 years of age; such a tender age to face a final blow to the heart, but his mama could not seem to contain her joy. The little boy was crushed, but not destroyed, yet. He began to grieve in the Oy Vey gevalt chutzpah while he grieved the loss of his father and the events of what he saw afterwards. He did not understand why his dad had to die thinking he did not ever do anything wrong to anyone.

In this son's eyes of his understanding, his parents belonged together; but in the "Divine Will" his father and mother had a law built upon lust. Lust is not of "faith!" How many times has it been read in the bible that part about "whomsoever the spirit joins together" let no man put asunder? There is a difference between the spirit and the law! The Spirit joins inlove…….the law assumes in writing; the spirit joins for life, the law gives mercy in divorce!

They had trespassed against the Spirit that made them, never having the conception of the spirit of faith in each other " joined inlove!"

They were spiritually wrong and sinning against the spirit. Without the spirit you can't please the spirit because you don't have anything from the spirit that belongs to the spirit! The spirit only accepts that which is *of* the spirit! When the spirit joins, there is no need to swear!

In the field there are wildflowers that that bloom and capture the beauty and give sap for the finest of honey, yet the purple coneflower, black-eyed Susan, blanket flowers, lupine, Indian blanket, Wild bergamot, Texas bluebonnet, Lance-leaved coreopsis cosmos, Mexican Hat, California poppy, Shasta daisy, Coreopsis, Columbine, Plains coreopsis, Zinnia, Wild lupine, Colorado blue columbine, Texas Bluebonnet, Aster, Pink ladies New England aster, just to mention more than a few!

Some you can just sprinkle the seeds; some were dropped by animal droppings that come back every year to bloom all the year round. This is true with wildflowers, but they are mere weeds to say the least.

A rose is a rose as with love, there is a difference between a weed being a wildflower blown in by a lust and gust of wind or do droppings than that of *the green thumb of the divine will of the spirit to give the gift of love!*

His father was good to his mother, but she was not his "Spiritual" wife; this young boy could not understand this truth, but like many of you will go to the grave without knowing the mystery of the conception of the joining of "Inlove!"

A "Divine Truth" that is a "Will" hidden deeper than his eyes could ever see at any time; there had never been a "spiritual conception of inlove" between his parents. Intercourse can't "join a man inlove to a woman for life, and neither will conceiving a child or giving birth to their child! Love is a conception of the spirit all its own, a gift that no one can give or stop or take away!

His parents were permitted to be tested of lust; proving by the "Faith of Love that nothing separates those joined by the spirit!"

"Love Wills" and *joins inlove* for *life*!

What did a little boy of 8 understand about this? Nothing!

He definitely didn't understand when mama and the pastor quietly continued seeing each other until even the pastor's wife died within a few months of his dad's death! Oy Vey Gevalt Chutzpah! Oh! My!

Nothing made sense to him at this point in life, by the time he was 10, Oy vey Gevalt Chutzpah rage took control of him, confronting anyone he saw in a fit of rage. Soon came the time when chance hunted him down; found himself landing in prison on his 18th birthday, staring at 21 years confinement for murder. His brother inlaw murdered his wife's brother; which was his big brother! Who ever read that charity begins at home?

Have you ever read your foes are those of your own household? This young boy felt he was his brother's keeper. He heard the preacher say that from the pulpit the very day before he shot his brother in law in the woods!

It was something that was bound to happen; this young boy was running from his own misguided childhood shadow.

He never understood the power of love and the destructional chutzpah of lust; he was conceived in a lawful marriage, but the law cannot give love; the law is not judgmental on whether you are joined or not..just sign and pay the fee!

The signature only holds you bound to pay that which you owe for the "taking" of what you were not " joined!" "One of you must "Die," If you can't wait for death, then divorce each other and live separate lives!

To free the other from the vowels of words spoken in haste until one of you dies still does not free you from the sin of swearing deceitfully!

21 years the man sat in prison hating his mother and praising his dad. He grew into a cold-hearted monster that sniggered at the pain of others, all the while crying inside when he appeared to be smiling. The harden man was released from prison bars of iron, but inside his mind was a cell; memories that locked him in remorse and resentment of Oy Vey Gevalt chutzpah!

He ended up marrying a younger woman that had 4 children from a previous marriage; she was kind of dumb and a little stupid too!

There is a big difference between stupid and dumb; knowing but denying is stupid, not knowing is dumb. It's not a bad thing to be dumb to the ways of the heathen; the bible states ___"learn not the ways of the heathen!" There would be another word for that kind of woman; naive! A naive woman is to be protected by her father and loved by her husband.

CHAPTER SIX

Chains that Bind With Lust of Hate!

This criminal finally took a law with *that* kind of woman; she was "dumb- cute," and this was what led her to her first husband and now being even dumber made the "Permissive ill" pause in their misguided life.

The woman was led astray with her stupidity; looking at men with the wiles of a snake but mistaking his wiles could be charmed by her being dumb and stupid.

What she saw was a man with cream colored skin, beautiful, good hair; he had a deep voice that was damaged by strong cigarettes and liquor. He was no different than her estranged husband; good looking only her husband had a body that danced to the music with every other woman.

He was a player that was unfaithful in marriage; being a father of 3 with one on the way didn't matter when he and his friends got together. This woman and man were a match and a strike together only to start a fire that would burn the wildfire of Oy Vey Gevalt chutzpah. There was never no love intended!

This is the very woman that was the mother of 3 other children; she was pregnant when she met this 2nd man that took her captive with the burden of lust, no deeper than the garden of evil allowed.

It was not important how the 2nd man used his bent-up lust towards the 2 young daughters and the first son of this young mother, but the barbarous cut of all is the mother denying it was or even happened.

All this mother knew was to deal with life like it never happened; she was molested by her own mother's new husband, and she remained silent as her mother to save this marriage.

This is the burden of lust; knowing something is wrong and remaining silent is making a path for more wrong. Two wrongs don't make a right: only paving another path for another victim. Silence is never golden when it's lust! Even the heart of compassion waxed cold!

The mother didn't want to talk or think about what she felt in her heart about her husband; instead appeared as if she could turn her face away from the Oy Vey Gevalt Chutzpah, as it became a weight that fell as a burden of lust on the oldest daughter first.

I will call her simply "the oldest sister," which by the time she reached 12, she began to seek attention from the only *male adult* in the house.

She was dumb; she liked the attention and the flattery that the stepfather gave her like most girls do. She began to grow to respond to his lusting smile and flattery of her dark skin.

She somehow knew something was wrong, but she couldn talk about what she didn't see about what had been going on in the secret corners for 4 long years. This was discernment, little did she understand what she felt was a spiritual sense, a gift of seeing without eyes!

There was her other sister and brother who knew of the activity between them and their stepfather, but things were somehow different now with her and this man.

As the years changed them into puberty, the 2 teenage sisters began to have a lust-hate relationship between them and their brother; they each were leading different lives that was getting heavier all the while to bear.

There would be fights that started just over being in the same room together.

The brother was having trouble sleeping at night; he would be caught sleep walking and the mother would see nothing wrong with this strange behavior in a 13-year-old boy. How can he walk in his sleep with his eyes closed ? He had a great sense of proprioception along with his equilibrioception and even his magnetoreception sense! Don't take my word for it ___ look it up for yourself! How many of you can close your eyes and walk around your house while awake without stumbling.. Now try walking in your sleep!

No one questioned the time alone spent with just the sisters and one brother in a shed with the stepfather.

The stepfather was relentless as he ruled his household with an iron hand. The molestation went on until the children grew up and the 2 older sisters left home; the brother was put out of the home when he turned 12.

CHAPTER SEVEN

Oy Vey Gevalt Chutzpah!

Lust continued to seek its victims; the victims becoming seekers and then the whole process repeats itself, spreading like a honeymoon of poison ivy blankets.

In the marriages of the 2 sisters; beautiful wives of men were glad to stake their future with, but even though the women were beautiful to lust upon the 18 senses they themselves were victims of also!

There was nothing they ever knew about love and nothing about being "inlove" do they know of today! It is impossible to live a lie with the divine will; it is not possible to deceive the other side of yourself, to your own self there is truth!

The joining of the conception makes the new life; it is truth, faith and joy of being inlove. Without being joined, there is no faith; without faith a man and a woman only have lust and cannot please the spirit with "lust" of the flesh! All that is in our senses are subjected to change with time and chance; only the divine will makes time work for us and not against us.

One of the 2 sisters has a story to tell of how much everybody loves her and how everybody wants to know her secret about how she has what she has: a wonderful husband and a daughter, a home and a comfortable lifestyle with friends.

Deep within her eyes there is a hint of sadness; a look that is hard to cover with a fake smile and manicured nails and coffered hair, denying she drank to make peace with the torment within her. She can't forget, she remembers every bit of the lie and deceit that has haunted her; she dranked and smiled that practiced smile with the squinting of her eyes that reached perfection, but never to her own heart was it true. That smile fooled some of the people some of the times, but not all of the people all of the time; and it never deceived the divine will!

Her stepfather has long been dead; her mother also, but they will never die within the unrest and guilt of her memory.

She never told her mother she was sorry; she never forgave the man who forced her and her sister to sleep with him and each other to satisfy his lust.

It probably wouldn't matter to her husband who is older now than her stepfather then when he died, but the burden of lust made her sick.

She lived her life the only way she knew how; she was dumb at first, but as she wised up, she became stupid. Stupidity has taken its toll on her life as it does in the end.

The 2nd sister took off in another direction down the crooked, but wide road that led to many deceptions. The paths of beautiful clothing and fancy dance steps that danced her down the wrong way. She hated her stepfather, another branch of lust that kept a deceptive cover; she didn't know how to love anybody as she knew she should. Life was full of confusion as she tried to find solace in the kisses and embraces of mostly every male that took her beauty for pleasure.

Her brother was a victim as herself and this became a bond between her brother and her sister; this was an evil bond, one that shared a weight of guilt and shame.

They had a baby sister; but this sister never knew the shame lived by them. This sister was always off with chores or visiting our Grandmother. The bond shared by those 3 older siblings became a wall, fencing them together in an Oy Vey Gevalt Chutzpah bondage for the rest of their lives.

The 2nd sister's husband honored her, his only wife of his 4 children; the first son was conceived he was told by him before they got married, He took ill then 38 years later needing a blood transfusion, before his death.

The oldest son was tested but was denied because his blood did not match his father's. The 2nd son that was named after his father was tested; it matched!

That should have been a happy ending; but he died after knowing the burden of lust, the very thing that plagued him for all his marriage was true! Oy Vey Gevalt Chutzpah!

Before he took this woman that was so beautiful to him to be his wife; unknowingly she was also beautiful to another man, she slept with him 6 weeks before and then became pregnant.

She laid the burden of lust upon the man that believed the baby was his; she knew it wasn't, she knew it all throughout the marriage of over 38 years.

Now that she didn't have to carry that burden of lust around any longer, she relaxed; but her grown son still wanted answers to questions that plagued him for as long as he could remember. "Why did he not have his father's name as a junior?" "Why did he look differently than his other brothers?" "What is the family secret?" His heart was searching for answers that only in time would reveal the hidden truth; the secret that would leave his life revealing a scar for revenge!

The burden of lust is a burden of guilt; it gets heavier and more cumbersome as time wears on. The 2nd sister is now a widow, and her son is a grown man of early 40's; a father with a son of his own, he wants clearance!

Like a circuit that will not be broken without consequences; the blessing of love is truth and honesty, but the burden of lust makes one weary. The son is searching for the identity of a father; but he finds that his father was one who was a stranger to him in his eyes.

He was tricked by the wiles of his mother; he couldn't see past the 18 senses as "The permissive ill" gave him a chance in time to meet his real father!

He was like a baby seeing his fingers for the first time; his eyes saw the person greeting him at the door; he was old and feeble, yet unlike a child the hands were not longing to reach out to touch this man that the resemblance that the DNA bore between them, but he stiffened them at his side in a tight fist then jammed them in his pockets.

They sat on opposite ends on his sofa with an oxygen tank and tubes feeding oxygen through his nostrils.

The son felt uneasy standing before his father; but Oy Vey Gevalt Chutzpah held nothing but the lust of pride, confusion and contempt.

The blessing of truth was something he searched for all of his life up to this very moment, now he finally found his real father, his eyes made him deny the relationship.

The father and son were separated by time, the DNA was there within them, but he used the sight sensor to deceive the mind; their blood matched, they sounded alike even had the same style shoes, but his eyes could not accept the tricks of time between them.

Both had grey hairs and a receding hairline which neither liked about themselves. They both had been married and divorced because of drugs and fast living with strange women of lust.

The son quickly changed his mind about who he wanted to be his father; but that did not matter, they were still father and son that were separated by lust!

He walked away from the truth knowing he had the same lust to bear with his own son.

He drove all the way home to another state, where his grown children carried the burden of lust in their generation.

He broke his children's hearts also, with a divorce from their mother years ago; the same lust that tore into him from his parents, Oy Vey Gevalt Chutzpah!

The spirit of unfaithfulness! Lust is not faith, it is fear, doubts and unbelief; *only the spirit gives faith in the joining of a conception of being inlove!*

This must be a family curse or something he thought as he grabbed him a cold beer out of the fridge as soon as he got back into his home state and tried to unrattled his brains from his emotions.

He had a feeling as if he had been hit in the pit of his stomach. He knew it all the time that he was different; he felt strange, yet it was an emptiness that he could not explain. It had to be that discernment sensor all the time; tipping him off to something deceptive that he could not see as a child, but he discerned it with his spiritual sense!!

He felt strange all his life with his brothers and sister and he wondered if the man he called daddy was really his dad; now he felt the same emptiness with the man that really *was* his father, but not his "*daddy!*"

How could he fight this hurt of losing something he thought he had when he never had it all along? How could he long for the truth all of his life and then it means nothing once he knew the answer deep inside all the time? Where was his happiness? He knew the truth, but freedom is strange when you don't accept it. He had nothing left to lose; he was free knowing who his father was, the man who raised him after all was the only *daddy* he knew!

Where was his father? He only felt sorrow, he felt he had been lied to and cheated all of his life; and he was right, he was!

The young man thought of his mother differently; she lied to him, she lied to everyone, but worse, she lied to herself all these years and she still is lying to herself blaming her baby sister for telling me the truth finally after 42 years!

Why couldn't she face the truth? She had no love! Love is the blessing of peace; all his mother had to give was lies and a burden of Oy Vey Gevalt Chutzpah lust!

His mind went back to his favorite Aunt; she told me the truth, she had honesty in her heart when she told him the truth, he felt her spirit.

Even though she held it in for over 42 years, she told me she knew that everyone in her family knew the truth except me!

They all kept this secret to not ruin the lives of two married people that had nothing but "lust" of the pride of life holding a law together that was full of anger, pain and mental suffering.

Now that the marriage is over in death, the children are grown; but the burden of lust still pressed down upon the heart with questions, this one son of the 2nd sister who lived under the burden of Oy Vey Gevalt Chutzpah lust.

CHAPTER EIGHT

The Sister Pushed Aside!

Why lust always ruin lives? No one wants to stop doing wrong!

Only when they get caught, maybe they will apologize, but too late to change the burden of lust and the damage it has caused.

The youngest sister hung up the phone. laid back in her bed knowing she did the right thing after her sister told her to wait until she was dead to tell her son the truth knowing that would have only been a cop-out adding to the pain!

Deception, the dark secret would be the link; a burden that this younger sister would not bear the guilt in her life any longer. The sister's oy vey gevalt chutzpah was a weak link in the family that was about to break loose in a chain of wildfires.

Sleep was sweet as morning came and she drank coffee in the light of her peace within. She knew what it was like to want to know her dad. The younger sister will always be the younger sister, but the burden of lust will not weigh upon her shoulders! She was not molested or knew anything about her sisters or brother being mistreated that way until they were all grown with children of their own, but now that she knew they were, answers came to her making sense to the questions that she had down through the years.

Actually I will share with you what my mother told me when I insisted that I wanted to find *my* real father.

I was about 13, old enough to see that my stepfather was never going to be good to me; I began to daydream about what it would be like to live with both of my paternal and maternal parents.

I waited until my mother was alone; "mama, I huddled close to her bedroom door watching her comb her long silky hair. I had not forgotten how I felt betrayed by her when I told her about my stepfather not treating me like a daughter. I never bothered to go to mama for anything personal since our first unsuccessful encounter; I didn't let that stop me from my desire to know about my real daddy. Mama was the only one that had real answers and I had to be the one to ask to get them from her.

"I know if my real daddy knew how my stepfather treated me, he would come and get me!" I felt so relieved to say those words that hung in my heart for at least as far as I could remember!

I waited for her to finally come to grips with what she wanted to say or if she would say anything to me about my daddy at all; she had the right to just tell me to never talk about him to her again, I was waiting for her answer as I searched her face with my discerning senses like I do to everyone.

Mama's face became pained as she looked directly into mine; she called my name, and these are the exact words she said to me.

"You don't know what you're talking about, you don't know him like you think; your daddy didn't love us when I told him I was expecting a baby which was you, he said to me I told you I didn't want *no* more of those things!"

Mama continued as if a flood broke a dam, and a flood of emotions emphasized her words while telling me my daddy left right after he found out I was in her belly!" Mama walked past me without saying another word; and I was silent, but my heart would never let me forget her words.

My daddy left my mama because of me; I repeated my mama's last words as she walked into the kitchen and out of my view.

I recalled seeing photos sitting on my grandparents wall. Several were of my parents sitting together with my 2 older sisters and my big brother.

They looked to be quite a happy family then, but I was not in that picture to be seen at *least*; I was in my mama's belly, and daddy hadn't been told about me being a fly in the ointment at that time.

I never was included in the photo; I was not wanted and not ever part of any pictures of my real mom and dad. I was out of their lives and daddy made sure of that.

I don't have to tell you I felt I was the fault of mama's divorce. Oh I finally wised up, but it would be years before I did!

I was the 3rd sister; the baby girl, the one that broke the family's back. I was just 14 when I learnt the details about my dad leaving, I began to see my life as a thing that wasn't wanted.

My daddy was the one who helped make me, he was the first one that proved how much he didn't care about me. I didn't have to learn anything more; the first and only man in my life hated me and that set the whole thing into motion about not being good enough for any man! Mama never had time for me; I was sent off to her mother's home every chance I had. I enjoyed being there. No one yelled or mistreated me in my grandparents' home.

There was plenty of everything, food, heat, and love. They loved me and I loved them. Of course I would try to tell my grandmother of the horrors that happened in my mama's house; grandma would tell me with a forlorn look in her face, unshed tears glazed over in her eyes as she simply said to me that my mama was grown.

"There was nothing she could do about what happened in my mama's life." I didn't understand why she felt that way, but I never asked her why; I never questioned any adult.

Grandma finished the last conversation we ever had on that subject with these words "I don't want to hear anything more about it!" She wasn't trying to be mean; she knew I understood it hurt us both to talk about what we could do nothing about!

I was young then when she said that to me; I learned to keep things to myself, over the next few years. I only looked and listened to the things that went on around me, judging them by the outcome on whether I should do it.

My grandmother passed and that left me terribly alone. I had to live my life constantly in my mother's home.

My stepfather, my 2 sisters and my 1 real brother; my 3 brothers that my mother had with my stepfather was a large family trying to survive without income. One of those brothers lived with my stepfather's mother.

Somehow, my stepfather didn't like his first son and refused to let him live with us. This son would be allowed to visit only for correctional purposes.

CHAPTER NINE

A House Divided Cannot Tolerate Peace

I was around 13 when this brother came to get a whipping for running away from his grandmother; mama never told me about this boy that called her Auntie!

Mamma was supposed to whip him, but when she pulled down his pants, she was horrified over what she saw.

"I can't whip you" I heard her whisper to him; how did you get those black marks on you?" Her voice cracking as the frail scared boy said, "Auntie that's where Grandmother whipped me!" I watched mama bend down, but not to keep looking at the boy's legs; she was crying and holding her hands over her face! I can't let you go through any more whippings! I heard mama tell this boy something that shocked me as I stood just outside the room , but within hearing still.

"I am not your Aunt; I am your mother!" The words came out of her mother, she could not call them back; she began to whimper with the tears from the burden of guilt.

Oy Vey Gevalt Chutzpah lust locked and infested deep inside her heart as the son she had turned her back on and neglected for 12 years also bore her burden with strips on his back to prove it.

I was not surprised at what mama told this boy that he was conceived by my stepfather; memories flooded my mind as it took me back 3 years ago when I was about 9 years old...

I was visiting my mama's mother; my grandparents in the spring of the year; they lived across the road to a park playground, where I was permitted to go swing as long as I was alone there.

After several moments alone, a scraggy little boy about my age with red, blond hair joined me in the park ground. He had a friendliness in his appearance as he ran towards the very swing set I was perched in; reminding myself of looking like a bird on a branch.

Immediately recalling my grandma's instructions, I jumped off the swing proceeding towards my grandparents' home. I could hear the little boy calling out to me in a cheerful voice "hey wild woman, where are you going to ___ come back!"

I didn't know who he was at that time, and the nerve of him calling me "wild woman;" I never looked back as I heard his continuing laughter at my long thick hair blowing in the wind!

I loved the feel of the breeze blowing my thick hair into my face and caressing my back like a scarf; I felt free and happy, embracing my image that I was made to have. I felt wild indeed ___ I felt free and happy!

I saw my grandmother at the edge of the yard; she was standing there watching the little boy and me all the while I was running towards her, suddenly she smiled down at me when

I reached her side asking me "why did you come back so soon honey?"

I then pointed to the little boy that was standing far off watching us. Grandma adjusted the rims of her glasses as she stared hard for a long time at the little boy then called the little boy over to us "come here!"

The little skinny boy wore baggy old clothes and dirty clothes like I wore at my mama's house, but at grandma's house I had beautiful clean clothes that smelled of lye soap and sunshine and fit me well.

Grandma adjusted her glasses as we both waited until the boy stood by our side. My grandma looked at him with an expression of endearment clouded over with a tinge of sadness; grandma asked him another question "Do you know who I am?"

The little boy and I exchanged glances of curiosity and wonder at each other; cupping our hands over our eyes shielding them from the glare of the sun. We both were spellbound looking up at the woman!

"Do you know who I am?" ___ We heard her repeat her question to the little boy. The little boy answered my grandma with a quick "No!" He had a note of laughter in his voice when he answered in a casual way. "I'm your grandmother!" Watching the face of both me and the little boy turn into sheer surprise, she asked the little boy another question; "Do you know who this little girl is?"

As the eyes of both me and the little boy met; we heard our grandmother tell us "we were brother and sister; we had the same mother; her daughter was our mother!"

At first the little boy took a step backwards and started smiling at me and our grandmother; then he said "come on wild woman let's go swing, take a swipe at my hair!" This was our first Oy Vey moment!

We never spoke about us being brother and sister as we played in that playground that day, but we both were thinking the very same things; we were brother and sister!

That wasn't hard at all; we believed we were brother and sister ever since!

I never saw this little boy again until after our grandmother on our mama's side of the family had died. The very one that introduced us for the first time is gone forever, but what she did would last between us for as long as we live as brother and sister.

He was now standing in the dim light of my mama's bedroom entrance; he stood with his back turned towards me, pants down around his bony stick like legs ready to get a whipping with a belt held in the hand of mama, our mama! Neither one of us recognized the other; we didn't know where each other lived.

We both knew we were brother and sister when we stood together in front of our grandmother, he didn't know who his mama was because he never saw his mama or even called anyone mama! My mama was keeping secrets until 5 years later, a little boy came into the house to get a whipping from his father and the woman he *called his Auntie* that day!

Even though a boy walked in my house, I never saw his face to risk getting a whipping too, so I hurried to my room, but I heard the words my mama spoke to him.We tried to put 2 and 2 together and still something didn't quite add up to a family for him and me when we thought of each other during the years we lived apart in different homes.

We never had the chance to recognize each other that day before he was sent back home to stay with his grandmother who beat him so badly. We both looked different; I had my hair braided up with dirty baggy clothes that belonged to my sisters, and he had been crying and was frightened out of his mind thinking he was going to get another beating from his Uncle-father and a woman that he called his auntie!

He was too young to understand how his uncle could be his father or even that I was living in the house where he would get beatings! At the time he came into the house, neither of us recognized the other!

We still lived in separate homes; children with 2 different fathers that didn't want us!

Neither of us saw each other again until time changed things nearly 2 years later. My stepfather's mother got too old to keep a little hardheaded, rambunctious boy such as my brother.

He was sent to live with his real mother and father and of course me, his sister! Of course we recognized each other, but we played our delight down; we knew never to act so happy about anything!

Mama and my stepfather never knew how our paths met years ago in the park as strangers, but stranger than fiction; our grandmother introduced us in the middle of an old country road, where the chance brought us together in a *"permissive will*! We were permitted to know we were brother and sister with the same mother!

I was 25 months older than this little brother; we were about the same size, malnourished and mistreated. We shared a wonderful sense of humor which kept us amused all the time.

We never went hungry, but we never ate good food; that was for my stepfather. I ate beans with no seasoning, no breads; I didn't know what a steak was and never had milk, or juice to drink.

We were not allowed milk or juice to drink; it was for my stepfather only. I love good cold milk! I would sneak milk occasionally in the middle of the night! I was only going to get just one cupful, that was just a sip, one swallow no one would miss that, nobody knew I did this, or so I thought...

I was not worried about doing my raid; one-night after all had gone to bed, my parent's light went out. All was clear to get some good milk! My mouth was watering as I tipped-toed into the kitchen and reached for the door of the refrigerator and opened it quickly, but the silence was suddenly broken!

A bright light shone in my face! Oy Vey! I felt like a deer caught in the street with the headlights of a car blinding me; then I heard his voice Ah-ha! I caught you wild woman! I caught the thief! You thought no one knew about you raiding the refrigerator at night, but I was watching you and I caught you, he teased!"

I stood stunned, papalized in the heat of the night in the spotlight of my brother's old flashlight beaming into my eyes with that stupid old alarm clock ringing like a police car in my ears! I felt pissed!

My brother had tied a string to the old rusty door handle of the refrigerator, the other end of the string was tied to the alarm switch; He then positioned the old alarm clock on the floor with the alarm set to go off when the string attached to the refrigerator handle was opened by me standing there caught about to reach for the milk jar _____ Oy Vey!

Mama and daddy both were wondering why that alarm clock was going off as my brother sat sniggering his little head off while peering at me through the entryway of the kitchen...

I scampered back into my room feeling like a rat caught in the trap by his tail. I began to think my brother was a nuisance, but my brother played games like that on me, often.

We laughed out in hysterics at him doing such a thing the very next morning as we scrambled and ate duck eggs from the weeds he found; he was my brother, and I was his sister!

Even though we had different fathers, we shared the same mother; different seeds but the same yoke starting as saplings in different homes now transplanted in the same soil together!

I spent many times wondering about things that took place in the house even before my little brother came to live with us, I did not talk to him about it; I never talked to anyone about the things that went on in my parents' house, there was no one who cared or could change things for the better.

One of the things I noticed was the way I was treated differently by everyone in the household.

I was used to my sisters and older brother talking privately all the time together but stopped just when I came around the corner.

I wondered why they were allowed to be in the playhouse with our stepfather and never with me!

Why would my sister think of herself better than her stepfather than mama?

Why would my big sister follow our stepfather around the house, sit on the arm of his chair, fix his food, serve his coffee and wash his feet, shave him and even kiss him on his lips before she left for school?

I had questions I never asked anyone to answer!

When he left the house, why would my sister pick arguments that oftentimes ended in fights between her brother who our stepfather had put out of the house by the time he was 12?

He hid in the darkened dampness of the cold dingy basement with our flea bitten hound dog! How could mama allow this to happen to her son? Mama was afraid of her husband, and this was something I thought I would never allow a male to make me feel.

CHAPTER TEN

Inlove With My Dreaman!

The divine will changed my life after my grandmother died; after her funeral, I returned to my parents that had moved to another place.

We now lived in a small old house that was made into a double; on both sides of the street gangs took over old abandoned double-homes and dogs barked constantly. There were old broken-down cars in the backyard being stripped of the metal to take to the scrap yard.

My stepfather joined in the stripping for his own personal gain for cigarettes and coffee money. He would cut metal and copper wire from the motor and the men would pay him to do this for them.

This became a daily job for my stepfather who would have us all in the back yard with pliers, etc. dismantling bits and pieces of metal to add up to a day's earnings. This was dirty and tiresome for anyone, but I was a young girl of 12 almost 13 and I hated the dirty greasy grime under my fingernails!

The children at school began to tease me and call me tom boy; I just hung my head and lowered my eyes and tried to block them out, it worked most of the time.

This is where my first incident happened that added to my mental anguish. Nothing happened, compared to what I later found out that my sisters and brother suffered.

My stepfather took advantage of me being in my bed alone; I shared a room with my 2 older sisters, this room was meant to be a dining room.

There were 2 walls that gave a plain view into the kitchen where the shadows of my sisters danced against the wall. Their voices sounded like low muffed music; they always had something to whisper about together lulling me to sleep each night. I often listen to crickets and even a mouse scampering under my bed as I drift off to sleep.

The bare light in the ceiling was a 25-watt bulb that was used only for the time they were doing the dishes then it would be taken to my parents room.

I liked the darkness when I slept; but as I slumbered my stepfather commanded me to get up and stand on my bed. No one had ever paid any attention to me before and this was a moment that only frightened me. He slid his hand down my pajamas while telling me "mama wouldn't give him any!" I had no ideal even at 12 what he could possibly find in my pajamas!

I wanted my grandma, but she was gone forever. It's strange how he waited until my grandma died before he ever tried to molest me! I would tell her for sure and maybe he knew that.

He smelled like cigarettes, coffee and body sweat all the time; this was no different as I felt the familiar fear rush over me in a most uncontrolled way. The only thing I ever felt around males was fear or nothing at all!

I began to tremble, and my voice just rose up in a strange sound; he told me to be quiet, but I was terrified beyond his control when suddenly in displeasure he began backing away telling me not to say anything to mama!

I will not forget the very next morning, a sunny Saturday; I heard mama coming into the back door, humming a church song. Mama grew up in the church, teaching Sunday School and singing in the choir.

We even had services in our home several times, so it was a way of life to live by the Bible and hearing mama singing all day long little songs that I knew the words to.

It was still early, around 8 am, everyone else was outside. I took advantage of the moment of privacy rushing up beside my mama as she was going to her bedroom which was the only bedroom in the double-4 room-shot-gun shack.

Often, I would sing along with mama, but this time I was not interested in singing as I scampered closer to her side carefully to keep an ear out for daddy coming into the house.

"Mama Daddy isn't treating me like a daughter!" I blurted out in a little scared voice, not knowing how else to say what I felt was wrong.

Mama continued walking until she came short of the entrance of her shared bedroom, her voice grew silent.

She was not singing, but she was not talking either as if she didn't seem to want to pay me any undue attention.

My ears picked up a familiar sound, my eyes trailed the pat-pat-pat; the sounds of mama's nervous habit of patting her head.

I discerned a coldness between us; I resisted this spirit not realizing it was there all the while, but I just became aware of it at the moment I brought up a subject that my mama had refused to believe existed with her even as a child. It was the same coldness I felt from my sisters and big brother. I pushed past the coldness, I hadn't expected it with my mama too.

I repeated my statement, and suddenly she stopped at the entrance of her room where the door was always closed; she half turned towards me, not looking directly into my face.

Her eyes darted off in another direction, as if searching for a convenient harbor to hide and shield her from the truth of my innocence. I watched her hand pat-pat-pat-pat-pat-patting her head in her nervous jester that made me feel irritated as well ___ she was trying to think of something other than what I had said to her; but in all reality, she was just trying to avoid this conversation all together.

She finally said in an empty, uncaring dismissive voice "I don't want to hear anything about it ___ if there's anything going on in this house that she needs to know about ___, the lord will let her know!"

She turned away from me as she opened her bedroom door, entered silently then shut the door in front of my face!

I stood there feeling a hurt I never recovered from. I was only 12 and a half, I didn't know anything about sex; absolutely nothing! I had never seen a boy naked, and I had no imagination to wonder what made a boy a boy different from a girl except only boys wore pants and liked to fight and hit me.

I knew then my mama didn't care for me; I knew I couldn't trust my mama and that meant that she didn't love me! How could she call what she just did to me love?

There was a distance between us even before that happened; but the distance grew to last until she died.

Oh, I tried to love my mama, but she always kept the distance between us; she was my mama regardless of how she treated me. I felt the same distance between all of my family members that lived in that house. We all shared the deoxyribonucleic acid from our mother, but we were distant relatives no doubt too close together!

It seemed that I was treated as an outcast, but in reality, we *all* were the outcasts from our own fathers; except my two younger brothers!

The 2 younger brothers knew what it was like to live with their maternal and paternal parents that stayed together until they died; but something was missing, mama was never inlove with no one!

I knew I wasn't loved by anyone but my grandparents, and after my grandmother's death, I never got to visit my grandfather until nearly a year later.

My 2nd oldest sister came with me to help our grandfather; he had diabetes, one leg and one eye was removed shortly after grandma died. Helping was not what my sister had in mind; she had a flurry of things to do that I see her do behind our parents back for as long as I could remember.

She used the time at my grandparents' home to contact the boys she liked. I was always told to be quiet and leave her alone with her kissing and hugging different boys in the backyard. Things were always like this with her, she was beautiful, and all the boys were attracted to her. I didn't notice how time was changing me as well; I was always watching everyone around me, but I never thought of how terrible I looked to other people; at that time, I was too young to notice and too unloved to care!

None of my family wore new clothes, there was nothing new in our house; we all took possession of things that were discarded. There was no such thing as possessions; I owned nothing but the skin on my back and I tried to keep my skin out of everyone's way!

My stepfather took my mama after she was deserted by my daddy, and I looked at myself as discarded by everyone in this family.

I continued going to school, church on Sundays; that became my lifestyle. I never wanted to be anything other than a wife and a mother of many children; but most of all I wanted to love and be loved with one man. I would be 62 years old before I would understand the "truth of being inlove!"

I wondered about many things as a young girl. I will tell you about the time when my 2nd sister invited a boy into the house after mama and daddy took our oldest sister to work.

I was 14 years old. My oldest sister was 20, my 2nd sister was 19; our brother had not lived with us since 12 was turning 18.

I was not only a virgin, but I honestly knew nothing about life in general. I didn't know where babies came from, and I didn't wonder where. I didn't know about the word sex or what it meant; I had not begun to menstruate, and I didn't know what that meant, because I never heard the word.

I was innocent. I had heard my stepfather refer to the "P" word to mama, I linked it to her private parts, but that was something that mama always was embarrassed about!

I was surprised by an older boy in the neighborhood grabbing and attacking me in my front room several minutes after my parents left home.

I managed to scare him off by screaming and shaking like I did with my stepfather; but this was only after he exposed himself then tried to open my pants!

What can you say to me when I know nothing at all about life? I didn't know where babies came from, and never heard the word "sex!" I was 14 in school, and this just went over my head; I simply daydreamed my troubles away, but this would be something I would get an answer from my sister ____ now!

Finally I called out for my sister, but she did not answer. My sister was busy in the back bedroom that we 3 girls shared, but with an older boy. Oy Vey! This was a shock to me as I saw both naked from the waist down and doing a strange kind of wrestling. I let the curtain close behind me that served as a door as I ran back through the house feeling bewildered!

My sister jumped up and let the boy out the back door and suddenly she was concerned about whether I was okay!

For the first time as sisters, she paid attention to me; "did he do anything to me?" This was the first thing she asked me." I was angry and frightened and didn't know what was going on.

"Why did she let those boys in the house while everyone was gone?" She only wanted to know what happened with me.

She asked me if the boy put anything inside of me; I looked at her with a blank expression that let her understand I didn't understand what he could possibly put inside of me. She still wasn't sure I had been raped as she quickly felt between my pant seam, then said with a look of nervousness in her eyes and heaved a sigh of relief "thank God he didn't do anything to you!"

I belted out at my sister ____ "What do you mean he didn't do anything to me ____ just hurt my arm and he tore my zipper ____ look?"

I stood there in my ruined pants that were faded and had holes in both knees; I asked her what was going on, that's when she told me what I thought was the craziest thing I had ever heard! She told me that if the boy put his privates inside of my privates, then that is how babies were made!"

I looked at my sister in shock, rubbing my sore arm and fumbling with my pants that had missing teeth in the zipper track.

I didn't believe her, I wanted to lash out at her for telling me such a silly outlandish thing! You're lying to me I lashed out in anger at my sister. I thought of how big babies were and there was no way they could squeeze into me by the privates of a boy!

She shook her head at my innocence and made me promise not to tell mama or daddy as she hurried and helped me take off my pants then took my pants and told me to find some more pants to put on. Those pants were the only ones I had!

We heard the old truck door slam and instantly closed that conversation to never come up again. That was never forgotten by me as my sister once more seemed to forgot I existed and went on seeing boys, only outside the back door.

I became an 8th grader that year and was told about reproduction; I didn't pay much attention but that didn't stop me from getting my first period.

I was so calm; I really didn't believe any of that stuff they showed me in health class, but not having any family member teaching me about menstruation; I went to my oldest sister telling her about the dried blood in my old underwear. It was a hot day in June, school was out for the summer; I was in the back of my stepfather's trash truck.

We had to go to the juvenile center because my baby brother didn't want to go to school, and he didn't.

My parents had to go to court, and I had to ride in the bed of the old dirty truck. Of course the people were laughing at me like the Beverly hillBillies, but what could I do about that? Nothing!

Daddy pulled into the driveway, and I was glad to get out and go to the outhouse. The bees and flies were always swarming around the old privy toilet. I opened the door and fought the insects as I pulled my pants down. They seemed stuck to me somehow.

There was this sticky dark burgundy paint like stuff stuck on my undies between my legs. It reminded me of spilt paint left to dry in the grass. I didn't think about what was happening to me as I pulled up my pants and went to my big sister.

I told my sister that something was wrong with me, I must have hurt myself somehow and I was bleeding. I never once thought of the films I was shown in school; I was in denial! I was living a life of denial while being denied!

She quickly peeped inside my underwear once in our bedroom and then told mama; mama gave me some old cotton cloth that came out of the back of my stepfather's trash truck. Mama didn't say much except that when I complained about what was happening to me, she said "you have to do this, you wouldn't be normal if you didn't!"

I wined saying "I didn't want to be normal." That was the only conversation my mama had over this subject and she never supplied any sanitary items; I was left to deal with it on my own, thank the school for toilet paper!

My stepfather was told by my sister and mama! He waited until he knew I was alone to tell me I was going to die! Why would my sister and mama tell him? I despised them all; I felt betrayed, my personal body function was nothing more than a nuisance!

CHAPTER ELEVEN

Within My Soul I Knew You!

I withdrew deeper into myself; my mama had no time for me, and I left her alone. I didn't mind reading and daydreaming my youth away, but somewhere within me after my period started there was an awareness of a man! I remember it precisely!

This man was different; he was inlove with me, inside of me! I became caught up with the way he would comfort me; he was I thought just a fantasy, but he was very much real to me!

Every night, and during the day I would be entertained by this man; no one knew about him, and I knew this man would be the one that I wanted to find in reality.

I poked fun at school and in the neighborhood among the children everywhere; even some of the adults would dislike me.

I became shy and introverted all the more, turning to my secret lover in my heart. He would comfort me; he knew how to do just that! No matter what happened in my life, I would always transpire every night in his embrace. He would say the right things and know how to get me to respond to him when I would not know how to do it the way I wanted.

My 2nd sister left home and soon my oldest sister prepared to leave within the year.

I was not prepared for what my big sister had in mind for me to do after she left.

Even though I now at 14 knew about how babies were conceived and also about how boys and girls were attracted to one another, I knew I wanted the man in my heart. I didn't know what he looked like, nothing about him other than he and I were made to love one another! This man was part of me and yet we were apart; I compared every boy to this male inside of me, everyone I met didn't measure up to the male that was loving me inside.

I was living in a daydream; I knew it, I also knew I had to live in a world where I struggled with just staying safe, warm and not bothering anyone

I was curiously aware of what made my oldest sister cling to our stepfather in the way she did; neither me or my 2nd sister did that, but nevertheless, she did until one of the neighbors made a statement about my sister going with her stepfather and this changed things!

My sister didn't tell me about this conversation, but the neighbor told me herself bragging about how my sister was doing that to her own mama's husband.

I was used to my sister serving our stepfather from childhood days; my sister would threaten anyone of us who tried to do anything that our stepfather would demand done.

By the time he had an operation that removed part of his stomach, he had to eat every 2 hours in small portions; mashed potatoes, salt pork, applesauce and bread soaked in milk.

Mama was busy around the clock and my sister fixed him coffee, serving him every 15 minutes! I was wearing my favorite blouse I found in our trash truck, cute little buttons on a tie front.

I was on my way to Sunday school when my sister came from the kitchen with a china cup steaming with black coffee and a teaspoon of sugar and cream; I stopped making sure I gave her space to pass me when she stopped in front of me and nearly shoved the saucer into my chest!

My eyes expressed a questionable doubt as they met hers that was filled with contempt; "here, take daddy his coffee and you better be good to him!"

She proceeded to walk away as I blurted out in resentment of possibly being late for church.

"What did I do to have this pleasure of serving the king?" My words fell on the floor as my sister was gone as quickly as she entered the room. My hands trembled; the fine China began chattering a high-pitched sound, I never held glass cups to take to my stepfather before now.

I knew he drank it boiling hot which made me move towards the direction of the front porch quickly. I thought he was sitting there waiting for his coffee I thought, but somehow when he saw me with his coffee, he began to smile.

"I brought your coffee daddy" I said, doing as my sister ordered and feeling uneasy, but as I lowered and offered the saucer with the cup clinging in both hands, he didn't take it.

I began that crazy trembling all over my body as I watched his hand creep towards me/ His fingers touched my pretty white pearl buttons that looked like little teardrops.

One thing I disliked about my blouse from the first time I put it on was the cute little smooth buttons that would never stay buttoned; mainly because they were too slick, and the eyelet was stretched, and the most important thing was the blouse was too small for me!

I began to breathe deeper than normal just as I felt one of those buttons slide open with the very touch of my stepfather's tobacco stained dirty weathered fingers.

I could feel the vibrations of my nerves and hear my mind scream for mama or my sister to come help me escape this moment, but no one came as I stood shaking while those fingers that resembled a spider groped behind my blouse.

I had been experiencing soreness around the brown area around my little nipples; nothing that could be noticed except that they ached.

Now with his fingers touching me there, it hurt even all the more as I was prompted by the pain to tell him "God does not like this ___ Daddy ___ God does not like this!"

I managed to get those words out that helped somehow because he drew his hand out of my blouse and in a pretended voice of displeasure asked me if I loved him.

He had tried to molest me when I was 12, now again at 14; I didn't know what it was called but I told him in a small voice that was forced out of my mouth "yesir Daddy, but this is not how you treat me as a daughter!" I was afraid of not standing up against him, not afraid of him!

He stiffened his back as he inched away from me and took his cup from my outstretched hand. I resisted the devil and he fled from me!

I backed away feeling my heart thumping within my chest trying to run with my body as I turned and opened the door without looking back.

I glanced over in the corner where my sister sat crouched in the chair; she had watched us the whole time, from inside the house from the window overlooking the porch!

This was a set-up! Both of my sisters had tried to set me up in order to carry out their own evil plans.

I escaped both times, but once again, I am reminded of that fact that I was not loved, starting with my real father and my mother and even my whole brother and sisters! If blood is thicker than water, my family must have had a jello transfusion!

My grandparents loved me, grandma was gone, and my grandfather was not allowed to see me. I learned so many things over the years after grandma died; I learned that my grandfather who was actually my step-grandfather molested my mama and her sister!

I never knew that! I didn't see that side of him, he was good to me and never made me feel uncomfortable in any way. I believe he loved me!

I woke up one morning in my bed alone; both sisters were gone, I was living here with my 3 half-brothers by my stepfather and mama.

I had to cut wood and break up coal for the front room stove that only kept my stepfather warm; I carried 2 5-gallon plastic buckets into the woods twice daily for water I drew up from the pump.

We had no inside plumbing, the pump in the woods had to be primed in the summer, unthawed in the winter; however I managed to survive the heat and the cold along with keeping my virginity from the big bad wolf.

All the cooking and cleaning was done by me at 15; life was all work and no play, but I had this male that was loving me inside.

CHAPTER TWELVE

A Dreaman WOKE Me Up

At the end of each day and the dark winter nights that was freezing and forlorn, he and I would whisper together; he would tell me how much he loved me and encourage me to be strong because we will be together one day!

I believed I would meet this man, I looked for the warmth and the understanding and the love that I was given in my heart by this special male; this male was hard to find.

I didn't know just how to find this male; he was only within me, but yet he wa*s soul* close and yet a *conception* away!

I continued to go to church and school and back home to work carrying water, wood, coal and housework; staying cautious in the house was always a thing to do.

I was not allowed a lifestyle like other teenagers; I never went anywhere; I did what I was told by my parents, borrowing sugar, salt, water etc. accepting the things that would cause me to be looked upon with disgust and pity.

I had been given something that at the time of my puberty that has been a guiding light; the male that loved me no matter what! I must say I always knew him, but where was he when I needed him in my real life? I married even before I graduated from high school; it was something that I did believing that the man in my daydream would only remain make believe in me.

I was in a battle with this daydream throughout this marriage; I realized I was inlove with a man that was not the man I was married to, but no one knew this.

I was never faithful to any man as long as I kept hearing this voice inside; everything I did with every man I married, I knew the man in my heart was who I really belonged to. I have gotten used to him in a way that I had never dared to reveal this part of myself to any other person.

I had 2 daughters by my first husband; I had no idea how to relate to anyone other than this man within me and he knew how to love me because he was in me!

I must admit my heart was never in the right place; my desire was that of someone that was too far to be touched, only his spirit could be felt.

I reached 25 years of age, and my first husband wanted more than what I was able to give; divorce was enabled after the 7th year. I had no plans to stop dreaming of this man within me; neither would this man stop appearing to me within my heart.

I got married for the 2nd time around; this marriage was no different, something was always missing even from the very beginning.

It was less than what I could speak of; I just didn't feel the way with either husband the way I felt with my dream love.

This 2nd marriage produced 2 more children and a sick relationship; it was sick to the core; I became a widow before the 7th year of marriage. I had a burden to lust that grew heavier with each marriage. My 3rd marriage hit me blindsided. I will not tell this story in this book, but it ended in divorce after 4 children and him nearly blinding and paralyzing me within 7 years before he deserted me.

I was trying to find love, not realizing that love is not lost. It is love that divinely chooses 2 people: joining both "inlove" together!

I had known my secret love; a love that let us know one another inside out, but I still promised to love men that my heart could never agree to even pretend to fool myself.

I never drank or did any kind of drugs; I was soon labeled as "unlovable!" By the time I was into my 4th marriage, I began to believe; I was unlovable. The man inside my soul had set a seal around my heart that I could not desire another man; I belonged to him and he belonged to me!

This 4th husband died from cirrhosis. Our marriage lasted 6 1/2 years before he died quietly with his departing spirit apologizing to me for the things he did because he did not love me anymore than I loved him. We were not inlove.

We were like a cat and a dog together; he would bark and corner me and I would hiss at him with my back against the wall. I could not submit to him without being "inlove!"

I married again for the 5th time; don't tell me about how 2 people born in the same month etc. is all that it takes to be lovers!

There is more to love than chance of date and birth; that is only part of the match, the most important of all is "divinity!"

I will not try to change my height or my eye color; but why would I do that? I cannot alter those things unless there was a major accident that required medical advice and even warnings of the risks involved in attempting to do so.

There is an anti-rejection medication for keeping your transplant, but against "love" there is no law that can stand against it!

There is an absolute law when it comes to love.

Love is a will, and a will is the power that controls the involuntary part of the brain; a brain has a mind of its own, that mind has a sensor organ that is divided into voluntary and involuntary responses!

There was an involuntary action of my brain controlling my most ardent feelings; the voluntary actions that allowed me to tell every one of my husbands the same thing and not be "inlove" with any of them! I knew in my heart, but my 5 senses deceived me! I ended up being divorced again; I finally began to accept that I was not loveable and that I should just be content to be happy with this dreaman.

The voice of my Beloved, I am his and he is mine! Let him kiss me with his lips, for his kisses are sweeter than wine.

His left hand is under my head, and his right arm embraces me. Do not arouse or awaken love until the time is right. Who is this coming up from the wilderness? Leaning on her beloved? Set me as a seal upon your heart. For love is as strong as death, its sparks are fiery flames, the fiercest blaze of all. Mighty waters cannot quench love; neither can the floods drown. If a man were to give all the wealth of his house for love, his offer would be utterly scorned. A man that is insecure learns to seek the praises of the world and his chosen woman will always be left behind never having him give her his quality time to spend together! A man that chooses the praises of men never has time for his own family; it's always someone else's needs he attends to. What does it profit a man to gain the whole world and lose his soul?

EPILOGUE

I choose not to tell you a lot of things; why do you need to know? I know what I know, I feel what I feel; I have what I have inside a secret place deep within the hypothalamus gland that is involuntarily turned on for the instance of a Spiritual Conception that connects the circuit of the two bodies flowing them with high levels of dopamine and a related hormone called norepinephrine together for the rest of their lives being "inlove!"

Finally, love has joined me to my dreaman; how? Again, why do you need to know? It's not about anyone but me and him which is actually all about "us!"

The voice of my beloved; I am his and he is mine, he is known within the gates.

For years we have loved this way; "Spiritually Connected," our circuits flowing together, touching and agreeing all these years! This connection has given us wisdom; our love is "Soulove!" We are blessed and highly favored to know we live our existence as we once dreamed, but actually we are not dreaming, we are living our dream!

Love begins within the spirit; by the spirit and of the spirit we grew, we matured in the faith. The blossoms of full blooming love took us both by surprise, "inlove" by the very Spirit! The sound of each other's voice is all the music we need!

The blessing of love or the burden of lust is truly the audacity of faith! Truly of all the people in this world, I am the woman; the one and only one and only that is one with this one and only man by the "Joining" and "Spirit of Conception."

There are 4 types of connections accruing within the nucleus of a circuit. "Inlove, intimacy, impregnation and birth."

1..."Spiritual Conception" O blood type
2..."Physical Conception" 99.9% of all
3..."Chemical Conception" pregnancy
4..."D.N.A. Conception" birth & maternal/paternal parents

1 ...."The Spiritual Conception"
The "Joining!" "The Awakening!"

Only the "Spirit Wills" an circuit to fuse into a conception between one blood type "O" man and one blood-type "O" woman. This conception does not start by physical conception but is sparked by the "Divine Will" joining those 2 people without their permission. This "Spiritual Conception" Divinely overpowers the "O" blood person's natural voluntary actions by a "Divine Will!" Without the Divine Will giving Faith, it is impossible to please him with the physical bodies that are subject to the common weakness of this world.

It is only being blind sighted not understanding the blood type "O" is "Divinely Willed" to reject anything that is foreign in relation to that person's <u>body, spirit and soul</u>; even to the point of fighting it off the skin, out of the body.

This "Divine Will" sends an oracle warding off people that are not in this "Divine Will" , keeping everyone at a distance.

<u>Why do you think a person is given "anti-rejection medication" for life to keep the body from rejecting a transplant even when it has been suited with his blood type?</u>

This divine will works its will in the joining of Soulove to blood-type O man and blood type O female only! O blood type man is "Divinely Willed" and not lawfully or voluntarily permitted to be with a woman of his own desires without a headache!

No wonder there are so many hospitals, liquor stores and prisons and a church on every corner.

The blood type "O" were not intended to be "inlove" with everybody, anybody, somebody or even just because you share the same blood type "O!" If you are an "O" blood type man, you cannot find your woman without "The Divine Will " Spiritually Connecting both Inlove circuits between you and 1 woman!

I must warn you, if you took a license with a woman before you are " joined," then you must understand you are "inlust" with a "strange woman."

Faithfulness is an attribute of being inlove; without the "Spiritual Conception Connecting" two circuits together, there is no joining, or constant flowing of devotion!

Love is faith; when The Spirit joins this man and woman of blood type O, then and only can they please the "Spirit with Faithfulness!" Faith is not of yourselves; it is a gift from the Spirit."

You are unequally yoked without this "Spiritual awakening!" There is no faith between you and any woman you have a law even if she is your blood type "O." Years being together, children or any other treasures you have stored up is not of faith if not given by "Faith!" Whatsoever is not of faith is sin! What is not of the spirit does not belong to the spirit.

The Spirit of Inlove divides the chosen from the ones that are not of "faith!" You can fool lust, but you can't deceive "The Spiritual Conception of Soulove."

Not only must the two be O blood type, but any and all lawful promises are treated as a spiritual sin; if either are in a law marriage with or without children, these relationships become true burdens and yokes of bondage until they are taken off one's shoulders by the Divine will!

All is fair in love and war; the war is a blood war; love is thicker than blood and the circuit between 1 man and 1 woman connected is at war against the world!

The Audacity of Faith in you & me; made us "one" from our "Spiritual conception!"

There is a chilling audacity to "divinity!" Divinity chooses who it will; when it wills, at its will! Divinity has no mind, it is "Will" Divinity never thinks, it knows, and Divinity is audacious and mind-blowingly surreal!

This is disturbing, but no more than any other factor that proves the marriage was built upon the lust of one's voluntary sensory action.

2... "The Physical Conception"

<u>The sexual act</u> between a man and a woman touching in an intimate skin to skin way. If this meeting is done by a common lustful beginning, there may or may not be pleasant feelings, but having sexual communication will not make anyone be "inlove together!"

Unless the two couples have experienced this "Spiritual Conception" creating a lifetime bond "inlove" will not exist between them by the lust of your desires.

Without this "spiritual conception," any meeting will be just a physical attraction of voluntary sensory lust.

All voluntary actions are subject to temporal changes that happen by chance in time; blood type O must shun and avoid all voluntary lust. Blood types other than "O" are humans that must use their common 18 senses to pick their partners and live with them as long as both agree in their lust for each other; divorce is their choice when their desires change, and it will! These groups are not bound to a spiritual conception of "Inlove" joining!

★"The Chemical Conception"
<u>"The Conception, Joining of the sperm and the egg
which is a chemical conception that is within the
body of the female. The D.N.A. Conception</u>
<u>The unity of the family at the birth of a child!</u>

There is a higher power within the soul of the O blood female that makes her submit to just one-man inlove for life!

There is a bond that is a circuit that will make one man cleave to one woman even though he is bound by law to another.

The law of love is written upon the hearts of those that are given the gift of "Soulove!" Nothing shall separate a man that is joined to one woman in the "Divine Conception of Soulove!"

For this cause shall a man leave his parents of the DNA born from the physical body of his mother; denying who-so-ever that is not of "Faith" and cleave to his "Spiritual Conception of whom they are Joined Inlove!"

This is marvelous in our eyes!

WORD DEFINITION

1...AUDACITY...Courage {absence of fear}-bravery-valor-resolute-boldness- confidence, manliness-spunk-grit- virtue- fortitude-firmness—stability-backbone-perseverance-tenacity-Joan of Arc;-defy-inspire-take the bull by the horns-go through the fire and water; run the gauntlet; go over the top; make a man of; keep in countenance; bold as a lion;-spirited-strong-minded,

2...BLESSING...Good-benefit-improvement-gain-world of good; harvest-happiness-in one's favor-children-gift-treasure; *whomsoulever* is joined together by the spirit.

3...BURDEN...A load, a weight typically a heavy one; a duty or misfortune that causes hardship, anxiety or grief, a nuisance. Pressing. Hardship or distress; an undue obligation to prove one's assertion; to bear; an ordeal or difficulty: A burden may be physical, mental, spiritual, financial or social; voluntary or involuntary, just or unjust.

4...CHANCE...Absence of assignable cause-indetermination-hazzard-luck-causality-random-contingence-coincidence-fate-probability-possibilility-odds-The possibility of something happening; the occurrence and development of events in the absence of any obvious design. The absence of any cause of events that can be predicted, understood or controlled. Often personified or treated as a positive agency. Chance governs all which is orchestrated by the Divine Will!

5...CHANGE...Alteration Difference at different times, mutations-permutation, Variation, modification, modulation, metastasis, mood, qualification, inflexion deviation, shift, turn, diversion, break, transformation, transfiguration; metamorphosis, metabolism, tranamutasion; metabolism, transmutation; transubstantiation; metagenesis, transamination, transmigration, from rest to action To make someone or something different; replace something with something else, especially something of the same kind that is newer or better, substitute one thing for another. The act or instance of making or becoming different. *_Extended lists are beyond the scope of this listing._

6…CIRCUIT…region; definite space, sphere, sphere of influence, corridor, ground, soil, area, head, circle, department, domain, territory, parish, tithing, kingdom, principality, commonwealth, state. A roughly circular line, route or movement that starts and finishes at the same place. A complete and closed path around a circulating electric current can flow. *_Extended lists are beyond the scope of this listing._

7…CHUTZPAW…A Yiddish word originated 1890-85 that refers to shameless boldness or almost-arrogant courage. Extreme self-confidence or audacity. Derived from the Mishnaic Hebrew word ``huspah meaning "insolence," or "cheek" considered a negative characteristic, along the lines of brazen nerve, impudence. Gall, conspicuous, flagrant boldness, effrontery. Supreme exaggerated self-opinion.

8…DEATH…Disease, demise, dissolution, departure, release, quietus, end, cessation, extinction; the action of one dying or being killed; the end of the life of a person or organism. The permanent ending of vital processes in a cell or tissue. Till death of our "hypothalamus" do us part! The physical release of one's spirit! *_Extended lists are beyond the scope of this listing._

9…DISCERN….*The spiritual gift to know God's desire in a situation or for one's life or identifying the true nature of a person, place or thing.; such as discerning whether a thing is good, evil, or may even transcend the limiting notion of duality. Spiritual judging the purpose, reasoning, outcome or positivity of a person, place or thing. judging whether to do or not to do it! To "cancel" the physical senses of the body, but spiritually sense what is hidden.*

10...DIVORCE...Separation, Moses's law, man-made death, judicial separate maintenance; widowhood, viduage, viduity, live separately, dis-spouse, put away, wear the horns. The legal dissolution of a "law marriage" by a court or other competent body. Dissociate, Split*_Extended lists are beyond the scope of this listing._

11...DIVINITY...Deity...Omnipotence, providence. Divine is "First cause." The Divine is "Author of spirit." Supernatural, angelic, mystical. Anything divine consists of divinity. *_Extended lists are beyond the scope of this listing._

12..DUMB...Ignorant, ignoramus, illiterate, moron, dunce, no scholar, dabbler, novice, learner, bungler, fool, shallow, simple, dense, thick, dull. Not showing or having good judgment or intelligence. Not knowing or understanding. *_Extended lists are beyond the scope of this listing._

13..FAITH... Spirit. Belief. A gift of spirit. Being pleasing to the spirit. The only way to please the spirit is by faith. Credence; credit; assurance; trust, troth betrothed, confidence, expectation, persuasion, self-conviction; certainty; conception. Conclusion, judgement, root. Trust, loyalty, dependence, dedication, fidelity, commitment, unshaken, dispassionate, impartial, reliance, certitude, credulity, adhesion, fastness, attachment, surety. Faith is a gift of knowledge to see and understand from the divine will of the spirit only! *_Extended lists are beyond the scope of this listing._

14..FULNESS-OF-TIME...Indefinite duration. Course, progress, process, succession, lapse, flow, flight of time. "Tomorrow and tomorrow and tomorrow creeps in this petty pace from day to day." The quality or state of being full. At some point; eventually. In due time, when the time comes, in the right time; after a due length of time has elapsed; eventually it will happen! *_Extended lists are beyond the scope of this listing._

15..GEVALT....-violence, shock, amazement. *_Extended lists are beyond the scope of this listing._

16..HOPE... presumption, optimism, castles in the air, fool's bliss, mirage, pandora's box, balms in Gilead. Entertainment, encouragement, presume, expect, look on the bright side of, on the sunny side, make the best of it, hope for the best, keep one's spirit's up, be of good heart, flatter oneself, lay the flattering unction to one's soul. Catch a straw, count one's chickens before they hatch. Give inspiration, inspire, raise expectations, reassure, buoy up, promise lookup, confidence, exultant, enthusiastic. Suspicion, distrust, despair, self-reliant, probable, good luck, never say did, all for the best, hope told a flattering tale. A feeling of expectation for desire for a certain thing to happen. Wanting something to happen or be the case. Wishing. Wanting something to happen or be true. Whatever the details, hope in general means a desire for things to change for the better, and to want that better situation very much. Hope is wishful thinking; the opposite of faith, an optimistic attitude of mind based on an expectation or desire of how things will turn out being unknown, Unseen without faith! *_Extended lists are beyond the scope of this listing._

17..HYPOTHALAMUS...The hypothalamus is a part of the brain that has a vital role in controlling many bodily functions including the release of hormones from the pituitary gland. The body cannot live without the hypothalamus gland; controlling the electricity to the heart's pulsating as well as the pull of chemistry connecting and joining "in-love" both are involuntary actions of the brain. *_Extended lists are beyond the scope of this listing._

18..ILL...Evil, harm, hurt, mischief, nuisance, machinations of the devil, Pandora's box, ills that flesh is heir to. Blow, buffet, stroke, scratch, bruise, wound, gash, mutilation; mortal-blow, damage, disadvantage, drawback, misfortune, calamity, catastrophe, tragedy, ruin, destruction, adversity. Mental suffering, outrage, evil doer, foul play, being in trouble, out of joint, amiss, wrong, Capability of producing evil, bad qualities. Virulence, plague-spot, evil star, ill wind; snake in the grass, skeleton in the closet; thorn in the side; Jonah, jinx, hoodoo, malignity; malevolence, tender mercies. Adversity, ups and downs of life, pressure of the times, bitter pill, trials and tribulations, hardships, not prosper, unblessed, hapless, in adverse circumstances, down in the world, on the road to ruins, on its last legs, ill fated, untoward, calamitous, unsuccessful, catastrophic, if the worst come to worse, as ill luck would have it, from bad to worse, out of the pan into the fire, the game is up, the ground crumbles under one's feet. Not in full health, sick, poor quality, badly, wrongly, or imperfect. Only with difficulty; hardly, a problem or misfortune. Vague illnesses you use "sick." more serious illness you probably would use ill. Under the weather, unwell, ailing, diseased, indisposed, infirm, off color, poorly, unhealthy, harmful, bad, damaging, deleterious, detrimental, evil, foul, injurious, unfortunate. Sickness, ailing, mortality, infirmity, aliment, indisposition; complaint, disorder, malady, distemper, visitation, attack, seizure, stroke, epilepsy, invalidism, delicacy, decay, malnutrition, decline, palsy, paralysis, prostrations, occupational diseases. Taint, pollution, infection, contagion, septicity, septicemia, blood poisoning, pyemia, epidemic; murrain, plague, pestilence, virus, pox. Sore, ulcer, abscess, fester, boil; pimple, swelling, carbuncle. Hindrance, prevention, proclusion, obstruction, stoppage, discouragement, resentment, displeasure, animosity, anger, wrath, indentation, vexation, exasperation, bitter resentment, bad humor, huff, virulence, heart burning, revenge, irritation, passion, tantrums, fury, desperation, gnashing of teeth, hot blood, high words. Offence: indignation, insult, grudge, slap in the face, lose one's temper, infuriate, bring a hornet's nest about one's ears. Violent, burning, boiling over, fuming, raging, convulsed with rage. *_Extended lists of "ills" are beyond the scope of this listing._

19..INVOLUNTARY...Unwilling. Indifference, done without one's will or conscious control, done against someone's will, compulsory. Done contrary to or without choice. Reflex. Cardiac and smooth muscle are involuntary. *_Extended lists of "involuntary" are beyond the scope of this listing._

20...JOIN...Connect. Junction, union, attachment, allegation, accomplishment, accouplement, marriage, communication, meeting, reunion, assemblage, chiasma, hinge, seam, stitch, link, closeness, tightness, coherence, combination, associate; put-lay-clap-hang-hump hold-piece-tack-fix-bind up-together-embody, roll into one. Attach, fix, saddle on, fasten, paste-secure, clinch, twist, make-fast, sew, lace, braid, harness, chain, fetter, hook, yoke, couple, solder, marry, bridge over, pin, nail, bolt, clamp, screw, fuse together; impact, graft, intwine, inter link, twine, weave, truce, be joined, hand in hand, intimately. A point at which parts of an artificial structure are joined. Where two become one spiritually. Connection of the electrical circuits between one male and one female for life. *_Extended lists of "join" are beyond the scope of this listing._

21..LAW...Regularity, rule, uniformity, clockwork precision; punctuality, routine formula; system, rut, canon, convention, keynote, standard, form, regulation, prototype, conformity, nature, principle, order of things, normal, ordinary, model, condition, procrustean law; law of the Medes and Persians, hard and fast rule. Statue, council, committee, court, chamber, cabinet, board, bench, staff, consultation, senate, parliament, House of Lords, Peers, legislature, legislative assembly, federal council, chamber of deputies, directory, divan, syndicate; court of appeal, board of control, works, vestry, county, borough, district, parish, town, council, local board, cabinet, privy, royal commission; cockpit, convocation, synod, congress, congregation, convention, diet, staters-general, aulic council. League of Nations, assembly, caucus, conclave, clique, conventicle; meeting, sitting, séance, conference, session, hearing, palaver, pourparler, durbar, pow-wow, house, quorum. Senator; member of parliament, councillor, M.P. representative of the people. Permission, leave; allow, suffer-once; tolerance, liberty, license, concession, grace; indulgence, favor, dispensation, exemption, release, connivance, vouchsafement, authorization, warranty, accordance, admission, permit, precept, sanction, passport; furlough, ticket of leave; grant, charter, patent, give, power, let, allow, suffer, bear with, tolerate, recognize, concede, humor, gratify, indulge, stretch a point, wink at, connive at, shut one eyes to. Enpower, charter, enfranchise, privilege, con a privilege entrust, sanction, *_Extended lists are beyond the scope of this listing._

22..LOVE...Obstinate, tenacity, perseverance, immovability, inflexibility, resolution, ruling passion, take no denial, have one's own way, unchangeable, involuntary, instinctive, compulsory, spontaneous action of the will of the spirit, uncontrollable. *Extended lists of "love" are beyond the scope of this listing.*

23..LUST... Materialism desire, wish, fantasy, want, exigency, mind, inclination, liking, fondness, impatience, passion, rage, greed, covetousness, mania, temptation, have an eye for, selfish, greedy, demanding, prideful, subject to time change and changes and 5 senses and self-control. *Extended lists of "lust" are beyond the scope of this listing.*

24..OY..."Oh, God" "uh-oh!" Enough already." *Extended lists are beyond the scope of this listing.*

25..PERMISSIVE...Allow, sufferance, tolerance, liberty, law, license, concession, grace, indulgence, favor, dispensation, exemption, release, connivance; warranty, accordance, admission, precept, sanction, authority, furlough, ticket of leave, grant, charter, patent, give,- permission, power; let, allow admit; suffer, bear with, tolerate, recognize, concede humor, gratify, indulge, stretch a point; wink at, cognitive at, shut one eye's to. *Extended lists are beyond the scope of this listing.*

26..PHYSICAL...Materiality, materialization; corporeality, -ality; substantiality, material existence, incarnation, flesh and blood, physical condition. Matter, body, substance, brute matter, element, protoplasm, plasma, parenchyma, material, substratum, hyle, corpus, pabulum; frame. Object, article, thing, something; still life; stocks, naturally – experimental- philosophy; physical science, embody. *Extended lists are beyond the scope of this listing.*

27..PRIDE...Loftiness, dignity, self-respect, haughtiness, high arrogance, high notions, hauteur; vainglory, arrogance, assumption, pom-posity, highflier; fine-gentleman- grand dame. Put a good face on; look one in the face; stalk abroad, perk oneself up; presume, swagger, strut; rear up, hold up, one's head; hold one's head high, look big, take the wall, bear like the Turk no rival near the throne, carry with a high hand; ride the – mount on one's high horse; set one's back up, give oneself airs. Take a pride in; hug oneself, be proud of;

not hide one's light under a bushel, dignified; stately; lordly, baronial; put one's talent in a napkin, haughtily; paughty, insolent, lofty, high, mighty, swollen, puffed up, flushed, blown; vain-glorious; purse proud, fine; proud as a peacock, Lucifer; bloated with pride. Supercilious, disdainful, bumptious, magisterial, imperious; high handed, and mighty; overweening, consequential; unblushing stiff necked; starch; perked stuck up- in buckram, straitlaced; prim with one's nose in the air. Full of one's self-worth and accomplishments; self-lust! *_Extended lists are beyond the scope of this listing._

28.. SENSES…Sight, touch, pressure, taste, sound, smell, itch, proprioception, tension sensor, nociception, stretch receptors, chemoreceptors, thirst, hunger, magnetoreception, time thermoception are our senses. A facility by which the body perceives an external stimulus. _The human sensory system is usually said to have at least 18 senses; hearing_ is the sense of sound detecting vibrations along some medium such as air or water that comes into our ears. _Sight_ is the sense of seeing thrones with our eyes of color and brightness. _Touch_ is the sense of feeling temperature, pain, texture with our skin. _Taste_ is the sensor of the flavor of sweet, salty, sour, bitter and umami based on chemical reactions with our tongues. Itch is a unique sensory experience in the central nervous system to elicit a characteristic behavioral response of scratching. Thermoception senses heat and cold. _Proprioception_ senses where your body parts are with eyes closed. _Tension-_ muscle tension. _Nociception_ senses pain in the cutaneous skin, somatic in bones and joints, and visceral in body organs. Equilibrioception senses balance and body movement, perceiving gravity. Stretch receptors are found in the lungs, bladder, stomach and the gastrointestinal tract. A type of stretch receptor that senses dilation of blood vessels is also often involved in headaches. Chemoreceptors detecting blood borne hormones and drugs; vomiting reflex Thirst sensor monitor hydration level, your body knows when to drink and tells you. _Hunger_ sense allows your body to detect when you need to eat something. _Magnetoreception is the sense_ of direction of the earth's magnetic field. Time sense. Danger sense detector to save your life. **Blood type O Homo sapiens have 2 extra senses: discernment of spirit.**

Emotional sense integrates with the part of the brain that stores memories. Discernment is the ability to judge by obtaining spiritual guidance and understanding; the quality of being able to grasp and comprehend what is obscure skill in discerning, In possession of one's faculties, senses! Loss of senses is loss of mind. Be sane; retain one's senses, reason. Physical sensibilities, sensitiveness, feeling, perceptibility, anaphylaxis, susceptivity, aesthetics; moral sensibility. Aware, responsive, alive to make a display of mouth honor, attract attention, put a good smiling face upon, pretentious, theatrical, dramatic display of one's senses. *_Extended lists are beyond the scope of this listing._

29…SENSORS… Eyes, ears, nose, skin, tongue, emotion are devices or sensors whose purpose is to detect the events or change in the environment such as heat, light, sound, pressure, magnetism, or taste, smell and respond to some output on the central nervous systems that respond back to the brain. *_Extended lists are beyond the scope of this listing._

30..SPIRIT… The intrinsicality non physical part of a person which is the seat of emotions and character, the soul. The Will that is unbridled, unconditional, immateriality, substance, quintessence, incarnation, gist, core, kernel, marrow, lifeblood, ethos, power, idiosyncrasy, to be born, derived from within, essential, inherited, coeval with birth, genite, indicative, invariable, incurable, ineradicable. Incorporeity, dematerialization, unsubstantiality, spirituality; in extension; astral plane. Immaterialism, spiritualism, subliminal, subconscious-self. Disembody, asomatous, unearthly, pneumatoscope. Fuel firing, combustible, tinder, brimstone; incense; match, wick, illuminant, candle. All things consist, nothing was made without the will of the spirit. *_Extended lists are beyond the scope of this listing._

31..SPIRITUAL…Immaterial, immateriality, immaterialness, incorporeality, dematerialization, unsubstantiality, spirituality; in extension; astral plane. Personality I MYSELF, ME; SPIRIT, IMMATERIALISM; SUBLIMINAL, SUBCONSCIOUS. DEMEBLODY, ASOMATOUS. *_Extended lists are beyond the scope of this listing_

32..STUPID...Unsubstantial, misjudging, credulous, unintelligent, thing of naught, man of straw, shadow; hollowness, blank; emptiness of mind. Ungrounded; having no foundation. Misjudgment, warped, miscalculation, hasty conclusion, whim, infatuation, blind side, mote in the eye, narrow minded, bigotry, estimate, think, conjecture, fly in the face of facts, overestimate, underestimate. Fore-judge, pre-suppose, have a bias, run away with the notion, jump, rush to a conclusion, view with a jaundiced eye, view through distorted spectacles. Having or showing a great lack of respect for intelligence or common sense. Knowing right but choosing to do wrong is STUPID!

33..TIME...Duration; period, term, stage, space, span, spell, season; the whole course. Intermediate time, while, interval, bit, pendency; cycle of life, age, year, date, decade, moment, instant, reign. The indefinite continued progress of existence and events, actions, or conditions exists or continues in the past, present, and future. A point of time as measured in hours and minutes past midnight or noon is recorded as a whole. Leisure, occasion, lifetime, season, turn, occasionally, eventually, frequently.

34..UNBRIDLED...Violent, berserk, fury, force, hysterics, outbreak, blowup, turmoil, tempest, be out of control, run high, wild, rage, amuck, make a riot, incite, irritate, infuriate, madden, add fuel to the flame; explode, displode, thunder, blow up, ungentle, boisterous, wild, victous; abrupt, rampant, rape, molest. Like a bull in a China cabinet. Like a bull at a gate. Uncontrolled, unconstrained lust.

35..VEY... "Oh, woe is me!"

36..VOLUNTARY...Overture, fore-runner, prelude, introduction, preparation, prefigurement, inaugural. Fantasia, movement, tweedily ditty, solo, base part. Done, given or acting of one's own free will; intentional, and deliberate means done or brought about, undertaken, etc. by choice, without being forced or paid to do it. Voluntary movement is the expression of thought through action. Virtually all areas of the central nervous system are involved in this process. The main flow of information may begin in cognitive cortical areas in the frontal lobe, or in sensory cortical areas in the occipital, parietal and temporal lobes. *Extended lists are beyond the scope of this listing*

37..WANT...Inferiority, subordinacy, shortcoming, deficiency; handicap; imperfection, shabbiness. Play second fiddle, take a back seat, bow. Weigh in the balance and found wanting; not fit to hold a candle unimportant, less; under, below the mark, at the bottom of the scale, a low ebb, a disadvantage, short of, under. shortcoming, insufficiency, shortcoming, failure, delinquency; failing short default, labor in vain, no go. Incompleteness, come fall-stop-short-within-of, not reach; stick in the mud, come to nothing; fall through, to the ground, down; cave in, unreached, out of depth perfunctory. Poverty, indigence, penury, pauperism, destitution, privation distress difficulties, wolf at the door. Embarrassed, reduced, straitened, circumstances; hand to mouth existence, beggary; broken, loss of fortune; requirement, need, necessities, stress, exigency, pinch, case of need – life or death. Desire; longing, solitude, yearning, aspiration, hunger.

38..WILL... Involuntariness; instinct, blind, impulse, imperiousness, fate, must be, destiny, inevitableness, will of the spirit, Thy will must, shall be done. *Extended lists are beyond the scope of this listing*

SUMMARY

The "Permissive ill" of the Spirit would allow one that is given by law marriage to obtain a right to bare or gain permission until things change for the better; the permissive ill gives you a permission to go against the grain, so to speak.

This is an excuse until you can do better waiting for a change to come. This permission can and should be done by signature only without opening your mouth.

Many war marriages were granted with just a signing of a signature without swearing verbally! Many unwed mothers were sent away to give birth to cover the honor of the family; "The Permissive ill" permitted this.

Have you ever read a sign that read "proceed at your own risk?" If you are being led by your own 18 senses; the permissive ill will allow you to have it your way; but the end results may not be desirable!

Many marriages were legally performed for the sake of sparing shame and disgrace upon the family; again, "Permissive ill" was given. This "Permissive ill" gives you an umbrella lusting for more when caught in times of a storm filled "chutzpah" life, but the "Divine Will" gives you a "Blessed" contentment of heart home; "Inlove" to live in and curl up in bed, while the storm of life passes over!

Another example of "Permissive ill" is your Doctor telling you there is no cure or treatment for your illness, but he gives you sleeping pills to make you comfortable while you languish in your condition getting worse. You are deceived and made comfortable with treatment that your immunity often rejects. Headaches, constipation, blood pressure and diabetes are warnings of being killed all day long like sheep heading for the slaughter.

In describing an example of the "Divine Will," The Doctor diagnoses an incurable disease, no cure and no treatment but the the next appointment the disease can't be found and was never treated by a doctor; and the disease never returned in that person's life!

Understanding the difference between "Divine" and "Permissive;" "Divine" is *totally permanent and unchangeable*, a *"spiritual occurrence before the 18 senses" can comprehend what has happened.*

Divine Will is an involuntary action that you do not choose, cannot change or alter; this will is not of your own doing in any shape form or fashion can you claim the Divine Will as your own doings, this is not a lottery ticket you purchase at a store! *The "Divine Will" only changes things concerning* **love, life, death!** "Permissive is being allowed an excessive freedom that normally would not be accepted by society or in a given situation at the time, but for a given period of time; liberty is given with "The Permissive ill" even without the legalities of the law can be given according to the "Will of the Spirit."

"Blessed is the man whose sins are covered!" "If The Spirit is for me, who can be against me?" "When The Spirit gives His "Divine Will " It is more than the whole world against me!

One more example: You get married by law and find you're not happy like 99.9 % of us have, but the "permissive ill" permits you to take an extra job; permitting you to stay out of the company of your law partner; but the "Divine Wills" a change in the marriage, your married partner dies, death is permanent! **The Divine Will simply "join" you** regardless **of a "legal marriage" love has no bondage, and nothing can stop the conception of the joining of lov**e!

"Divorce is a "permissive ill," ending a "paper-right;" permitting both persons to live separated, continuing intruding in the future with paternal and maternal rights of their children. This is "dysfunction in action; lust was at its beginning!

Divorce is what the Oy vey gevalt chutzpah of lust does when it is just beginning to make you shake your head in disbelief! Only "death" ends a life permanently! This change will be forced without any person, place or thing being able to change it.

I must add that the "Divine Will" is not subjected or led to follow our ways; when the "Divine Will" alters our lives, it is not for a vain thing, it is only about the things that are of the Spirit!

The "Divine Will" intercepts our deceptions of our 18 senses! The "Permissive ill" allows or permits a chance in time to prepare our 18 senses for the shock of our lives receiving the divine will that we can't change! or direct us as the "Divine Wills" people, places or and things At the right times using our 18 senses or the common laws of the people! It may allow us to wait for a change, or it may permit us to pass by something that would hinder us in the future.

The "Permissive ill" is different from The "Divine Will!" Time is limited in the "Permitted ill;" allowing one to be patient and wait. In other words, there is a time to mend and heal; to root out and pluck up. There is a time to cast away stones and the Spirit permits this time at its own "Will" not ours,' but we think we are in control when we are not, if it is "His

Will," we will do this or that! Time is on your side in The "Divine Will," granting something right now! The "Jointing" of 2 people is a "Divine Will" action; "inlove" happens "Right Now!" It is permanent; unchangeable, unconditional, lasting a lifetime.

There is time for all things under the sun; a time to love, a time to laugh and a time to dance. Love is a spirit that lives in the soul; deeper than the emotions, "Willing" changes that chance upon our lives through time.

There is a time for lamenting in mourning, casting away stones from the heart. Pride of life with all of its vainglory must come to a halting end, but love born forever in the soul of a man and a woman abided forever. Love embraces only its own; draws bodies together regardless of the consequences or sacrifices!

The people who are bound by lust will continue to lust until they die unless they are "joined in Spiritual Love together." All is fair in love and lust, asking no questions of "why?"

Where there is truth, there is love, joy, peace and blessing of contentment. Where there is deceit, is the root of lust and every evil burden; Oy vey gevalt chutzpah!

Neither turns into the other; love never wants, "love has;" lust "is the spirit of wantons," because it never has the peace of contentment!

Here in this book, the lust of the eyes and the pride of life runs rapidly destroying glass houses built with the hands of the 18 senses; sand foundations that crumble during the changes of time upon chance.

From the view of one family and the burden of lust that has a far cry from the blessing of love until one woman is joined to one man.

Unlike lust, love joins; it is the circuit that flows along with the beating heart, staying as it is "Divinely Willed" to do.

The blessings of love or the burden of lust is just a part of life having a will of its own against the mind that is led by the sensors that are limited to deception.

Love or lust, blessing or burden? Love is an audacious "Will;" lust is an Oy Vey Gevalt Chutzpah sensory; at its best, temporal, subject to chance and change over the course of time.

To love or not; only the "Divine Will" builds the foundation upon the modest blessing and the audacity of love between one man and one woman for the rest of their lives spent "inlove together!"

AUTHORS NOTES

My Beloved's Voice woke me Up! Oy Vey! What did I know about "love?" "Nothing!" "What did I know about being "inlove? "Nothing!"

I signed my name on paper swearing to the world with a void that was not going to be filled. I looked at every man, no smiles, no kisses and nothing that could hold a candle to the "Dreaman" within my soul! I trespassed against my spirit; became a truce breaker, walking in the console of the ungodly; sitting in the seat of the scornful; feeling the same old feelings of emptiness. I was used to it; it was all I ever had, an empty bed and me curling up with no one other than my dreaman! He always comforted me; he knew how to reach me where I was one with him together. He had no face that I could see, but we knew each other's pain and shared each other's passion.

Being "inlove" is everything and more than I could ever ask or think; there is love after all, but it is not what, where and in what one would ever think.

Being "inlove" is the birth of awakening from being by oneself and suddenly you're not alone, but "Inlove" with the only one that is the other half of yourself!

Happiness plays upon any uncertain fleeting moment of lust; but joy is the laughter of being "inlove for the best of our lifetime!"

The unseen power of being joined is being suddenly awakened from a separation of the love that was once together spiritually, but by the connecting of our electrical circuit between us; we became one.

There are many things I am not willing to tell you, but you could not believe me; your human mind is made to reject that which you cannot wrap your "common-walk-around 18 senses around!"

I will just be talking over your head, then too, "why do you need to know?" You knowing, cannot stop whomsoulever the spirit hath joined together! My love and I have been joined in the faith of love; a conception continuing to be heads-over heels-in love! What I see with my physical sight is insulting and my thoughts are dishonoring and belittling to the spirit within me. More than I am able ___ I am blessed! How blessed am I? I know the spirit blesses me beyond anything that I am able to ask or think according to the power that works within me ___ so I study to be still and be blessed!

Norah G Wilson
A.K.A._____ authorladynorah.com

ABOUT THE AUTHOR

NORAH G WILSON; a uniquely distinguished Spirit encased in a jewel box! One who delights in the things unseen and unheard by the common physical 18 senses! Norah has been granted according to the Spiritual Glory an "Inlove" Conception; a Gifted strength of Faith being Enjoined by Within the Realms of Soulove! Being rooted and grounded in "Inlove," of whom the whole family in the Spirit is Joined, knowing the Love of the Spirit which passeth knowledge, being filled with all the Fulness of the Spirit. *The most Exquisite moment that Joined her in a Spiritual Conception, started with just One Moment in time sealing Two Into One; Lasting the rest of Their Lifetime!* Norah G Wilson enjoys her passionate ability to express this comprehension in her writing and singing; creating the music that expresses overflowing joy from the love which passeth knowledge, filled with all the fullness of the spirit within her soul. AuthorLadyNoraH.com enjoys the breadth, and length, and depth and height that only the "Conception of the Joining of Two bodies' Into One can experience!" NorahgWilson.com holds other power-filled books by this author; her literatures, scripts and music also may be purchased at Barnes and Nobles, Amazon, Xlibris.com and AuthorLadyNoraH.com and Booktrails.com

SPECIAL SPIRITUAL THANKS

Now unto the Divine Spirit that is able to Will and Do Exceeding and Abundantly above all that we were able to ask or think according to the power of the Divine Will that worketh Within Us, Our Cup Overflow Inlove without End!

My Beloved and I give thanks!

AuthorLadyNoraH.com

CPSIA information can be obtained
at www.ICGtesting.com
Printed in the USA
LVHW031546251021
701446LV00001B/217

9 781637 673829